BIG TRUTH LITTLE BOOKS®

SOLOMON'S GREAT COMMISSION
A THEOLOGY OF EARTHLY LIFE

Derek Brown

WITH ALL WISDOM PUBLICATIONS
Cupertino, California

SOLOMON'S GREAT COMMISSION
A THEOLOGY OF EARTHLY LIFE

Solomon's Great Commission: A Theology of Earthly Life
Copyright © 2019 Derek Brown
Published by WITH ALL WISDOM PUBLICATIONS
Requests for information about can be sent to:

Publications@CreeksideBibleChurch.com

ISBN: 13: 978-1-7336041-5-4

Solomon's Great Commission: A Theology of Earthly Life is volume 15
in the Big Truth little books® series.

General Editor: Cliff McManis
Series Editor: Derek Brown
Associate Editors: J. R. Cuevas, Breanna Paniagua, Jasmine Patton
Proofreader: Sergio Gonzalez
Cover Design: Oluwasanya Awe

To P. J. Tibayan and Rick Zaman
Men who have taught me that much laughter and
serious discipleship go well together

CONTENTS

SERIES PREFACE

Our mission with the BIG TRUTH little books® series is to provide edifying, accessible literature for Christian readers from all walks of life. We understand that it is often difficult to find time to read good books. But we also understand that reading is a valuable means of spiritual growth. The answer? Get some really big truth into some little books. These books may be small, but each is full of Scripture, theological reflection, and pastoral insight. Our hope is that Christians young and old will benefit from these books as they grow in their knowledge of Christ through His Word.

Cliff McManis, General Editor
Derek Brown, Series Editor

INTRODUCTION

In the academic year of 2017-18 I took our college students through a study of the Old Testament wisdom literature. We began in Proverbs and eventually made our way to Ecclesiastes. While I had read Ecclesiastes several times in my regular treks through the Bible, that year with the college students was the first time that I had thoroughly studied the book. What turned out to be a very challenging study actually came to yield significant fruit in my own life and, judging from the responses I received, in the lives of the college students.

It was shortly after I completed this study through Ecclesiastes that I decided to preach through a small portion of the book to our church body. The section I chose for the sermon was a collection of four brief verses that had stood out to me during my study and teaching that had subsequently embedded themselves into my mind and heart. I couldn't escape the glorious and life-giving implications of what these verses were teaching, and I wanted to share these insights with the greater church body.

In the weeks leading up to the week I was slated to preach, people would inquire about my topic or text. I told them I was preaching from Ecclesiastes 9:7-10 and Solomon's command to enjoy earthly life. I was particularly excited to preach this text, and I told the people who asked that it was going to be an encouraging sermon.

I was especially excited to preach on this text because it had become clear to me over the past few years that Christians, by and large, do not have a robust theology of earthly life—myself included. On the one hand there seemed to be Christians who, in obedience to Christ's command to "deny themselves" (Luke 9:23), were tempted to approach earthly pleasures with a deep-seated suspicion or outright rejection.

On the other hand, there were believers who seemed to be displaying little distinction from unbelievers with how they appropriated and, let's be honest, indulged in what we might call the good things of life. Somewhere in the middle were those who recognized that neither extreme was probably right yet who were without a complete biblical framework to help them square Scripture's call to holiness with a world that seemed to be bursting with pleasure and opportunities for enjoyment.

Ecclesiastes had done much for me to clear out some legalistic overgrowth from my own heart, and establish a more full-bodied theology of creation and earthly enjoyment. There was now less dissonance between the biblical call to self-control and self-denial, and the immensely pleasurable world in which I found myself. I hoped hearing from Solomon would have the same sanctifying effect for others.

The response I received from the sermon was encouraging. People mentioned that they were helped by Solomon's exhortation to enjoy this earthly life as a gift, and how such a call could be (and should be!) incorporated into a life devoted to glorifying God and pursuing holiness. A few months later I had the opportunity to preach this same message to a group of brothers at a men's retreat at a church in Virginia. The response at this men's retreat was again positive, and a brother even asked if I was thinking about turning this message into a book.

Due to the spiritual benefit I have derived from Solomon's words in Ecclesiastes 9:7-10 and the way I have seen Scripture encourage believers on this topic, I have decided to expand these thoughts into a slightly longer, more detailed, and readable format. I am convinced that Christians will benefit from a thorough meditation on the topic of earthly enjoyment, so I have sought to provide readers with a careful reading of Ecclesiastes 9:7-10 in light of its immediate context and its broader theological context.

Since the time I have taught and preached on this passage, I have gathered some more research to supplement my reflections and to clarify points that I was unable to address in previous expositions.

Nevertheless, this book still retains a simple structure and format.

Chapter 1 establishes our text in the broader context of Ecclesiastes and helps us understand how Solomon viewed the world. This chapter sets the stage for our exposition of Ecclesiastes 9:7-10 in chapters 2, 3, 4, and 5. Chapter 2 is a reflection on Ecclesiastes 9:7 and Solomon's call to savor life joyfully. Chapter 3 is a study of verse 8 and Solomon's admonition to maintain a posture of celebration throughout one's life. Chapter 4 is a meditation on Ecclesiastes 9:9 in which we will find Solomon's exhortation to enjoy life thankfully. Chapter 5 reflects on verse 10 and Solomon's command to live our lives with zest and intentionality. In each chapter we will discover an underlying plea to enjoy our earthly lives.

Before we explore these verses, however, it will be necessary to fit ourselves squarely into Solomon's world and acquaint ourselves with the troubles he had uncovered in his life under the sun. Ironically, in order to rightly appropriate biblical teaching on earthly enjoyment, we must first reckon with the state of this world and its inherent limitations. We now turn to these considerations in chapter 1.

1

SOLOMON'S GRAND DISCOVERY

Ecclesiastes is a book both familiar and unknown. Even if a person has never read the Bible, it is likely they have heard phrases from the book of Ecclesiastes. The declaration "There's nothing new under the sun!" is an expression that has made its way into our collection of English idioms, and it comes directly from Ecclesiastes 1:9:

> What has been is what will be, and what has been done is what will be done, and there is nothing new under the sun.

Solomon's poetic reflections on God's providential ordering of life and its seasons can be found in a host of American cultural artifacts—from funeral programs to throw pillows.

For everything there is a season, and a time for
every matter under heaven:
a time to be born, and a time to die;
a time to plant, and a time to pluck up
        what is planted;
a time to kill, and a time to heal;
a time to break down, and a time to
        build up;
a time to weep, and a time to laugh;
a time to mourn, and a time to dance;
a time to cast away stones, and a time
        to gather stones together;
a time to embrace, and a time to refrain
        from embracing;
a time to seek, and a time to lose;
a time to keep, and a time to cast away;
a time to tear, and a time to sew;
a time to keep silence, and a time to
        speak;
a time to love, and a time to hate;
a time for war, and a time for peace (Eccl 3:1-8).

Yet, while a few of its phrases may be recognizable, the
book on a whole is unfamiliar to most people—even
many Christians—due to difficulty in interpreting
significant portions of the book. While a few broad
themes in Ecclesiastes can be grasped rather easily (e.g.,
Solomon sought ultimate meaning in the pleasures of
this life but found them to be unfulfilling), many

sections are downright hard to understand. I realize that maybe only a handful of those reading this book have studied Ecclesiastes in depth, so we need to take some time to get our contextual bearings before we get to Ecclesiastes 9:7-10.

The first thing we need to say about Ecclesiastes is that it was written by King Solomon, most likely at the end of his life.[1] In this book, Solomon offers his readers hard-learned wisdom grounded in his observations on earthly life. Having departed from God's law shortly after he was installed as Israel's king, Solomon found himself mired in sensual indulgence and spiritual idolatry. Contrary to God's instructions for Israel's kings (see Deut 17:16-17), Solomon accumulated many wives and concubines, a vast and powerful military, and wealth that surpassed the affluence of surrounding nations. His sin, however, led to Israel's eventual spiritual, political, and material decline. In response to Solomon's departure from the Law, God split the people of Israel into a northern and southern kingdom and allowed corruption to retain a foothold on most of the subsequent leaders.

Before he died, however, Solomon came to his senses. He had sought ultimate meaning and satisfaction in earthly pleasures and used every resource he had at his disposal to acquire whatever he wanted, but it couldn't slake his thirst. Yet in his search, Solomon was forced to look unflinchingly at life with all of its sorrow, monotony, joy, enigmas, and frustrations. He had to ask some difficult questions about the providence of God, the pervasiveness of suffering, the prevalence of injustice, and the place of pleasure.

Thankfully, his wandering and restoration were not in vain. Through his sin and disillusionment, Solomon learned a few vital lessons about life under the sun: four observations that he now offers to us so we might walk in wisdom during our brief pilgrimage on this earth.

Observation #1: There is Nothing New Under the Sun

Solomon's first observation is that there is nothing new under the sun.

> What has been is what will be, and what has been done is what will be done, and there is nothing new under the sun. Is there a thing of which it is said, 'See, this is new'? It has been already in the ages before us. There is no remembrance of former things, nor will there be any remembrance of later things yet to be among those who come after (Eccl 1:9-11).

What has the old king realized thus far in his earthly life? He has concluded that life is repetitious on both a macro-level and a micro-level. We experience this macro-level monotony in the seasonal changes: winter, spring, summer, fall; winter, spring, summer, fall. We also notice there is a kind of unbreakable monotony when we consider life from a historical perspective. One commentator describes it this way:

> Earthly existence does not consist of an unending series of discoveries—going where no man has gone before. Yes, there are things such as nuclear power and manned landings on the moon that never happened in prior history, but the vast majority of events are merely repetitions in a slightly different costume. There is a constant yearning for new things and new experiences, and yet, what is new for one person is old hat to someone else. Try as we might, we cannot change history.[2]

Earthly life prompts us to constantly look for something novel and out-of-the-ordinary. History teaches us, however, that we are unable to locate anything that's actually *new*. A few remarkable human discoveries and achievements may make it appear that we've finally broken the cycle of monotony, but even these innovations leave us dissatisfied and longing for more. Even the appearance of newness when humankind develops new forms of technology (e.g., flight, space travel, nuclear power, iPhones) quickly gives way to the reality that life is still the same. People are still sinful, and our world is still fallen. While annual graduation speeches speak to the contrary, the attempt to "change the world" is futile. "What is crooked cannot be made straight, and what is lacking cannot be counted," Solomon laments a little later in his introduction (Eccl 1:15). All the inventions in the world are unable to alter the basic fabric of reality or push humankind beyond the wearisome repetitiveness of life under the sun.

Tedium afflicts on a micro-level as well. You wake up in the morning, eat breakfast, go to work, come home, eat dinner, and go to bed. And then you wake up the next morning and repeat the same routine for the next sixty years of your life. On the whole there is a cyclical repetition in life that, among other things, prompts Solomon to cry out: "Vanity of vanities, all is vanity" (Eccl 1:3). In other words, the maddening reality with which Solomon must reckon is that there is no novelty that can break into his experience or get him beyond this cycle of earthly life, or what one has called "the fatigue of monotony."[3]

Observation #2: Ultimate Pleasure, Satisfaction, and Meaning Cannot Be Found in the Things of this Life

The second observation is that earthly life cannot provide people with ultimate satisfaction and purpose. In response to the bewildering monotony of life, Solomon conducted an experiment and sought to break the cycle of despair by seeking ultimate satisfaction and meaning in earthly enjoyments. "Perhaps," Solomon thought, "ultimate meaning and satisfaction and pleasure are found in intellectual stimulus," so he sought after wisdom and knowledge: "And I applied my heart to know wisdom and to know madness and folly. I perceived that this also is but a striving after wind" (1:17).

But he soon realized that intellectual stimulus didn't bring him definitive satisfaction or pleasure or meaning. Why? Because the more you learn, the more you realize what you don't know, and the goal of achieving comprehensive knowledge of the world and all of its mysteries becomes pure fantasy. What about sensual pleasure? Solomon tried that, too:

> I said in my heart, "Come now, I will test you with pleasure; enjoy yourself." But behold, this also was vanity. I said of laughter, "It is mad," and of pleasure, "What use is it?" I searched with my heart how to cheer my body with wine—my heart still guiding me with wisdom—and how to lay hold on folly, till I might see what was good for the children of man to do under heaven during the few days of their life (Eccl 2:1-3).

But he couldn't find ultimate meaning or satisfaction in sensual pleasure, either. Laughter and fun tend to merely serve as a diversion to numb oneself from the hard realities of life, and pleasure by itself cannot change the fundamental character of the world. "What use is it?" then, Solomon asks. Where else might he turn for ultimate satisfaction or meaning? Perhaps he should look to more noble pursuits than mere sensual pleasure? How about work and productivity?

> I made great works. I built houses and planted vineyards for myself. I made myself gardens and parks, and planted in them all kinds of fruit trees. I made myself pools from which to water the forest of growing trees (Eccl 2:4-6).

Yet, even in an area of life that constituted an essential aspect of Solomon's design as an image-bearer— productive labor (see Gen 2:15)—he still couldn't find what he was looking for. The aim of his productivity might reveal why he found work so empty: Solomon confessed he built houses and planted vineyards "for myself."[4] Whatever the reason, none of these aspects of earthly life—intellectual pursuits, sensual pleasures, and productivity—could fill the void that Solomon felt in this life under the sun.

Observation #3: Death Comes to All People

Solomon's third observation, and perhaps the most bitter of all, is that death is certain and afflicts all people. Whether you are rich or poor, wise or foolish, nobility or peasant, your earthly status and wealth cannot impede the certainty of death. Death levels all people, irrespective of who they are or what they've done:

Then I saw that there is more gain in wisdom than in folly, as there is more gain in light than in darkness. The wise person has his eyes in his head, but the fool walks in darkness. And yet I perceived that the same event happens to all of them. Then I said in my heart, "What happens to the fool will happen to me also. Why then have I been so very wise?" And I said in my heart that this also is vanity. For of the wise as of the fool there is no enduring remembrance, seeing that in the days to come all will have been long forgotten. How the wise dies just like the fool (Eccl 2:12-16)!

Solomon, however, is not only bewildered by the pervasiveness of death; just as distressing is the fact that you are quickly forgotten by the next generation: "seeing that in the days to come all will have been long forgotten." Only a fractional number of people are remembered long after they have died. Among those is an even smaller percentage of people whom history considers worthy of regular commemoration. For those who were never close to the recently departed, life moves relatively quickly from grief to normal routine. Daily remembrances turn into monthly reflections which turn into passing yearly thoughts. Eventually, the deceased are remembered by only a small few, usually only family members. Whether you are a fool or wise, death will eventually visit you, and history will not remember who you were or what you did. These conclusions brought Solomon deep despair to the point where he finally said, "I hated life" (Eccl 2:17).

Observation #4: Life is Full of Enigmas

Solomon also observed that life under the sun is full of enigmas. An enigma is something mysterious, puzzling, or otherwise difficult to understand or make sense of in your present experience. When Solomon takes an open-eyed look at life, he observes aspects of our earthly existence that are completely beyond our figuring out.

How is it, Solomon asks, that people are oppressed and no one is there to comfort them (4:1)? How is it that a righteous man perishes in his righteousness, and yet a wicked man is allowed to prosper and prolong his life (Eccl 7:15)? How is it that people are subject to death, regardless of their social, religious, or moral status (Eccl 9:2)? It doesn't matter if you're religious or irreligious, morally respectable or totally corrupt; death comes to all people. Furthermore, life is unpredictable. "Again I saw that under the sun the race is not to the swift, nor the battle to the strong, nor bread to the wise, nor riches to the intelligent, nor favor to those with knowledge, but time and chance happen to them all" (Eccl 9:11).

From an earthly perspective, Solomon concedes that there is no one-to-one formula we can rely upon that says, "If you conduct your life in this way, you will achieve this or that guaranteed outcome." The race often goes to the swift, but what happens if the best runner on the track trips and falls halfway through the race? Nor does the battle always go to the strong. Occasionally an event might occur within a particular military situation where a stronger army is ambushed and defeated by a lesser army. Nor does the bread always go to the wise or riches to the intelligent. You may have a Ph.D. and yet be struggling to make ends meet or homeless because you've been overtaken by an addiction.

Due to his glum observations, it might be easy to view the author of Ecclesiastes at this point much like a sophomore-year philosophy student going on a rant about the meaninglessness of life. Yes, Solomon is grappling with the truth that life from an earthly perspective is unpredictable and difficult and confusing, but he is *not* doing so as a cynic. These are not the jaded words of a pessimist; they are the sober and wise reflections of a man who has been brought to look unflinchingly at the harsh realities of life. When we are honest, we must admit that there *is* monotony in this life; there *is* the question of where ultimate satisfaction can be found; there *is* the pressing and impartial reality of death; and there *are* many enigmas that we cannot solve this side of eternity.

Clarity in the Confusion

But that's not the whole story, is it? Throughout Ecclesiastes Solomon mingles hope with despair, moments of confusion with glimpses of clarity. Although we cannot unravel all the riddles of life or figure out what God is doing in the world, we can know *some* things for certain, and these things stabilize us in the midst of this fallen world.

First of all, Solomon knew that God is sovereign over all events and all people. The familiar passage we noted earlier in this chapter is rather profound and even vital for understanding Solomon's outlook on life. As he considers God's providential ordering of earthly life, Solomon tells us, "For everything there is a season and a time for every matter under heaven" (Eccl 3:1). That's not just a flowery platitude: Solomon is arguing that because God is sovereign over all things, there is a time and place for every event that transpires on this earth, and He has all the providential details carefully arranged in His plan. But, just as important, God has arranged the providential details in such a way that we cannot, with our finite perspective, discern all the specifics. Nevertheless, under God's sovereignty, there is a time and place for everything and He has it all under control. You may not be able to understand the particulars of providence, but God is ruling nonetheless.

The Place of Pleasure

Here is another important piece of the puzzle that Solomon has put in place. The old king also knows that God has given mankind earthly life as a gift. For those who reject God and do not know Him, the good things of this life are pursued as ends in and of themselves. Earthly enjoyments—food, drink, marriage, pleasure, work—are pursued as the items that hold ultimate satisfaction and meaning. But because these things are sought as the source of lasting satisfaction *in place of* the Creator, rather than enjoyed as temporary gifts *from* the Creator, genuine satisfaction becomes elusive. If you look for the infinite in the finite, Solomon says, you will be disappointed every time:

> There is an evil that I have seen under the sun, and it lies heavy on mankind: a man to whom God gives wealth, possessions, and honor, so that he lacks nothing of all that he desires, yet God does not give him power to enjoy them, but a stranger enjoys them. This is vanity; it is a grievous evil (Eccl 6:1-2).

This reality rattled Solomon's brain. A person can have access to the most exquisite pleasures this world has to offer, and all the resources to acquire whatever he or she wants, but apart from God these things turn into sand. We don't need to search very far to find anecdotes that confirm Solomon's observation. Stories of lottery winners whose lives fall into ruin shortly after their financial windfall; celebrities who take their own lives while seemingly relishing every pleasure this world has to offer; wealthy couples who live in misery and bitterness despite their earthly riches; and world-class athletes who wonder openly about the meaning of life after they've acquired countless on-the-field accomplishments are all examples of those who possess great earthly advantages but do not possess the power to enjoy them.

Nevertheless, throughout Ecclesiastes, in between Solomon's observations of the enigmas and difficulties and sorrows and troubles of life, he returns multiple times to this subject of earthly enjoyment. This emphasis on earthly pleasure is rather ironic, given some of Solomon's conclusions we've already noted. Although he has discovered that earthly life cannot give him *ultimate* satisfaction, Solomon learns that God has created life to give us *some* satisfaction, and he repeats this theme multiple times throughout the book:

> There is nothing better for a person than that he should eat and drink and find enjoyment in his toil. This also, I saw, is from the hand of God, for apart from him who can eat or who can have enjoyment? For to the one who pleases him God has given wisdom and knowledge and joy, but to the sinner he has given the business of gathering and

collecting, only to give to one who pleases God (2:24-26).

I perceived that there is nothing better for them than to be joyful and to do good as long as they live; also that everyone should eat and drink and take pleasure in all his toil—this is God's gift to man (3:12-13).

So I saw that there is nothing better than that a man should rejoice in his work, for that is his lot. Who can bring him to see what will be after him? (3:22).

Behold, what I have seen to be good and fitting is to eat and drink and find enjoyment in all the toil with which one toils under the sun the few days of his life that God has given him, for this is his lot. Everyone also to whom God has given wealth and possessions and power to enjoy them, and to accept his lot and rejoice in his toil—this is the gift of God. For he will not much remember the days of his life because God keeps him occupied with joy in his heart (5:18-20).

And I commend joy, for man has nothing better under the sun but to eat and drink and be joyful, for this will go with him in his toil through the days of his life that God has given him under the sun (8:15).

Intermingled throughout Solomon's hard look at life under sun—with all of its monotony, trouble, enigmas, sorrow, oppression, and inequities—is the constant refrain that earthly life is a gift to be enjoyed. Neither his realistic outlook on life or his experience of pleasure's limitations draws him into asceticism or the rejection of God's gifts. Rather, as we will see in the next few chapters, Solomon will take the opportunity to strongly urge us to receive these gifts with gladness and gratitude. We turn now in the next chapter to consider Solomon's first exhortation.

2

SOLOMON'S GREAT COMMISSION

SAVOR LIFE JOYFULLY

Go, eat your bread with joy, and drink your wine with a merry heart, for God has already approved what you do.
Ecclesiastes 9:7

Solomon had given himself to searching where he might find ultimate meaning and satisfaction in this life, yet he had come up empty. As we saw in the last chapter, however, his discovery didn't turn him into a grumpy misanthrope. Rather, he began to grasp the place that pleasure has in the life of the believer. Earthly pleasure isn't the main thing, but it isn't to be rejected, either.

Yet, what's stunning about the passage we are examining in this chapter and the next two chapters is that up to this point, Solomon has only commended joy. He has said things like, "there is nothing better" (Eccl

2:24) or, "behold, it's good and fitting" (Eccl 5:18) or, "I commend joy" (Eccl 8:15). These statements are observations and suggestions. But by Ecclesiastes 9:7-10, Solomon becomes far more aggressive: he now *commands* you to enjoy life.

What's interesting about this passage is that it is inserted in between 9:1-6 and 9:11-16 where Solomon grapples with a few of the most painful mysteries of life. In 9:1-6, Solomon reckons with the reality that death is certain and eventually visits all people, regardless of their moral or religious status. In 9:11-16, Solomon observes that life is often unpredictable: the race doesn't always go to the swift nor the battle to the strong. In light of these painful realities, the question Solomon seeks to answer in 9:7-10 is this: How do you, as a believer who knows and loves God, navigate this painful, unpredictable life? How do you endure life under the sun? This is how:

> Go, eat your bread with joy, and drink your wine with a merry heart, for God has already approved what you do. Let your garments be always white. Let not oil be lacking on your head. Enjoy life with the wife whom you love, all the days of your vain life that he has given you under the sun, because that is your portion in life and in your toil at which you toil under the sun. Whatever your hand finds to do, do it with your might, for there is no

work or thought or knowledge or wisdom in
Sheol, to which you are going.

Notice the first word in this passage: "Go" (9:7a). Does that sound like something you've heard before (see Matt 28:18)? Life is full of difficulties and enigmas and troubles and things that you will never be able to figure out this side of eternity. So here is Solomon's instruction in light of these truths, and it's an urgent matter: "Stop your worrying and fretting about things you cannot control and that you are never meant to figure out, and go, Christian, get on with living this life that God has given you." As one commentator has put it: "The first command is 'Go!' It's a wakeup call. There is no time to waste. Stop your complaining. Stop nursing your anger. Stop brooding over your problems. Get over your anxiety."[1] In other words, start enjoying the gift of earthly life.

Again, what's astonishing about Solomon's statement here is that it is a *command*. He has given us a moral imperative to be followed, and we all know God and our Bibles well enough to know that to disobey a command is *sin*. Obedience is not optional. "Instead of allowing grief to consume one's life, Solomon urges that whatever remains of the unexplained mystery in our lives must not prevent us from enjoying life. The tendency to brood and to mope about has to be resisted in the lives of those who fear God," one commentator reminds us. He continues with an admonition, "…take life as a gift from his hand, and receive God's plan and enablement to enjoy that life."[2]

But what, specifically, are we to *go* and do?

Eat Your Bread and Drink Your Wine

Solomon's first command is for us to *savor life joyfully*. "Go, eat your bread with joy, and drink your wine with a merry heart, for God has already approved what you do" (Eccl 9:7). In other words: find enjoyment and pleasure in eating and drinking. What a command! When you are freed from the tyranny of having to find *ultimate* satisfaction in food and drink, you can find *some* satisfaction in food and drink, and that is exactly what God intends for His people.

But we also need to consider what else Solomon says in this text. Why should you eat your bread and drink your wine with a merry heart? Solomon gives a surprising reason: "For God has already approved what you do." What does this mean? Is this a license for unrestrained indulgence in whatever I want? Does this statement mean whatever I do, God approves it by the sheer virtue that it originated from my own volition? No. Such an interpretation would implicate God in approving wickedness, which is impossible (see 1 John 1:5). Wholesale approval of all our actions is not what Solomon is affirming here. Rather, he is revealing his robust theology of creation.

God's First Command to Humankind

If I were to ask you, "What is the first command in the Bible?" what would you say? You might say, "Be fruitful and multiply," (Gen 1:26) and that would be a good answer. However, in terms of chronological sequence, the command to be fruitful and multiply would have come later because Adam was created first before the woman, and the command to be fruitful and multiply is given to the man *and* the woman (see Gen 2:7ff; cf. Gen 1:26).

Let's refocus the question: What was the first command given to *Adam*? You might say, "You shall not eat from the tree of knowledge of good and evil." But is that the first command? Let's look a little closer. "And the LORD God commanded the man, saying, 'You may surely eat of every tree of the garden, but of the tree of the knowledge of good and evil you shall not eat, for in the day that you eat of it you shall surely die'" (Gen 2:16).

The first part of the command is God's instruction to Adam to *enjoy the food that God had created for him to enjoy.* The reason why many of us would have answered that the first command was "you shall not eat from the tree of knowledge of good and evil" is that we are still breathing the lie-tainted air that Satan introduced to our spiritual atmosphere six millennia ago. The first command God gave to His human creatures was a command to enjoy the abundant goodness of creation. The lie that Satan introduced to Adam and Eve was that

God was *keeping enjoyment from them.* Consider the content of the Serpent's temptation. "He said to the woman, 'Did God actually say, "You shall not eat of any tree in the garden"'" (Gen 3:1)? Satan's strategy was to flip God's commandment on its head in order to make it appear as though God was primarily a prohibitor of enjoyment rather than a glad provider and proponent of it!

Yet, given our connection with Adam and Satan's ability to subtly influence our own thinking, we must ask: Is that how I think of God? I fear that deep down some of us conceive of our Creator in this way. That is, there may be a good number of us who hear God speaking primarily in terms of prohibitions; we simply assume the first command was *not* to do something because that's how we naturally think of God.

But this text in Genesis teaches us that God actually initiated His relationship with His human creatures with a command to enjoy what He had provided. Far from standing against His creatures as a prohibitor of pleasure, God's first move toward His people is to lavish them with every conceivable holy enjoyment. He has created this good world for the benefit and the delight of His creatures. When Solomon commands us to savor life joyfully because God has already approved what we do, he is taking us back to creation and showing us that legitimate, earthly pleasures were given to us by God for our blessing.

Think of it for a moment. God made our bodies to require food in order to grow and thrive, and He could have provided for our daily sustenance by fashioning some kind feeding apparatus that we plugged directly into a tree or plant in order to absorb its nutrients. But He gave us *taste buds*. The conclusion Solomon wants us to draw? Go, savor life joyfully!

Whatever You Eat or Drink

Bread and wine were staples in Solomon's day, so the immediate reference is to the enjoyment that can be found in eating and drinking. The application, however, is not merely to bread and wine; it is to whatever you find yourself eating or drinking.

My wife and I have traveled to Ethiopia on multiple occasions to complete two of our adoptions. Coffee is a staple in this part of the world, and there were coffee ceremonies at set times of the day in which we were regularly invited to partake. The coffee is rich, dark, and very good. Ethiopian cuisine is also very delicious: a combination of flatbread and berbere-seasoned stews; traditional Ethiopian fare has become a favorite in our home.

Several years ago, I traveled to New Zealand with a group of fellow Christians to minister to a church in Wellington. It went without saying that at least two times a day we would gather for tea and a light snack. And to this day, whenever I drink lightly-sweetened English Breakfast tea, I am often transported to my time in New Zealand. In New Zealand the drink of choice is tea. In parts of the U. S. it's a frosty soda. In Ethiopia, it's coffee. Solomon's point is not to restrict our enjoyment to bread and wine, but to say that in *whatever* you eat or drink, do it with joy and with a merry heart (cf. 1 Cor 10:31). Eating and drinking are God's gift to you, and He is pleased when you enjoy these gifts and thank Him for them.

Let's get specific. When you bite into that fresh Fuji apple chicken salad, or that perfectly prepared filet mignon, or that moist piece of peanut butter cup chocolate ripple cheesecake, or that spicy salmon roll, or that ripe Bartlett pear; or when you sip on that perfectly brewed vanilla latte or that vintage Cabernet and you savor and enjoy it and you thank God for it, He is pleased. He has already approved what you do.

What About Self-Denial?

Perhaps you recoil from the implications I am suggesting at this point. "We live in a society that is bent on consumption and over-indulgence," you object. "How can you command us to savor food? You should be exhorting us to self-control and to self-denial so that we might be lights in a dark world!" Well, that objection may sound spiritual and humble, but it could actually be rooted in self-righteousness and a deficient understanding of the gospel. Let's be clear: the answer to sinful over-indulgence is neither abstinence nor the rejection of God's good gifts.

Paul addresses this very problem in his letter to the Colossians. Apparently, there were false teachers in Colossae who promoted a brand of religion that resembled Christianity and appeared exceptionally holy but actually grew out of a denial of Christ and a rejection of the gospel. These false teachers and proponents of their doctrine would say that true religion was kindled and expressed by denying oneself the basic pleasures of life, and they would pass self-righteous judgment on the Christians who freely ate and drank, looking down their noses at the Colossians' supposed lack of holiness.

Paul emphatically rejected this kind of approach to God and exhorted the Colossians to hold their ground. These Christians were not to allow anyone to bring them into the bondage of asceticism, nor were they to embrace any teaching that outlawed legitimate pleasure for the sake of so-called holiness:

> Therefore let no one pass judgment on you in questions of food and drink, or with regard to a festival or a new moon or a Sabbath. These are a shadow of the things to come, but the substance belongs to Christ. Let no one disqualify you, insisting on asceticism and worship of angels, going on in detail about visions, puffed up without reason by his sensuous mind, and not holding fast to the Head, from whom the whole body, nourished and knit together

through its joints and ligaments, grows with
a growth that is from God (Col 2:16-19).

While it may not initially seem as strange or incongruous
with biblical religion as angel worship, Paul warns the
Colossian church that the same people who promote
asceticism are the same ones who engage in blatant
idolatry and have detached themselves from Jesus
Christ. Both idolatry *and* the denial of legitimate
pleasures God has already approved are the result of a
diminished view of Christ and salvation. Paul continues:

> If with Christ you died to the elemental
> spirits of the world, why, as if you were still
> alive in the world, do you submit to
> regulations—"Do not handle, Do not taste,
> Do not touch" (referring to things that all
> perish as they are used)—according to
> human precepts and teachings? These have
> indeed an appearance of wisdom in
> promoting self-made religion and asceticism
> and severity to the body, but they are of no
> value in stopping the indulgence of the flesh
> (Col 2:20-23).

The Christians in Colossae had, as Paul notes, "died to
the elemental spirits of the world." While it is difficult
to know exactly all that Paul means with this sentence,
the context gives us enough light to draw enough sure
conclusions. On the whole, Paul's main point is to

remind the Colossians that they have died to *superstitious spirituality*.

To participate in the "elemental spirits of the world" is to partake in religion that is natural to our fallen human condition. On our own, we tend to think *wrongly* about God and what He requires of us. When we don't know the Creator and the truth that He has provided us with complete forgiveness in Christ by grace through faith alone (Eph 2:8-9), we constantly seek to allay our guilt through self-atonement. This self-atonement comes in many forms, but the specific expression Paul addresses here is the tendency to assuage our conscience by participating in asceticism, severe treatment of the body, and by rejecting certain foods as unholy and unspiritual.

These gospel-less exercises, however, have absolutely no power to produce genuine, heart-level change in anyone who practice them, nor could these activities bring people into closer relationships with and experience of God. Usually, these strident, superstitious attempts at holiness enflame our sinful nature and cause sin to explode with greater force in other areas of our lives. Those who understand the gospel know that Christ is the substance of true religion and recognize that food and drink are good gifts from our Creator to be enjoyed.

Yes, let's admit it. We live and work in a society that celebrates over-indulgence and leverages most of its energy and resources to acquire and consume earthly pleasures. But as *Christians,* we know that this world is, though fallen, still good. And, as Christians, God has not only approved what we do on the basis of creation, He has approved what we do on the basis of the gospel. In Christ, we are declared fully righteous and free from condemnation at this very moment! There is no need to earn God's favor through abstaining from certain foods or rejecting legitimate earthly pleasures. In Christ we are free to enjoy the good things of this life in the way they were intended to be enjoyed.

What about 'Don't Be Anxious'?

But perhaps you have in mind another objection to Solomon's exhortation. How can I make such a bold statement, you wonder, in light of Jesus' straightforward instruction to not worry about what we eat and drink? That's a fair and thoughtful objection. But let's look at Jesus' words in their entirety:

> Therefore, I tell you, do not be anxious about your life, what you will eat or what you will drink, nor about your body, what you will put on. Is not life more than food, and the body more than clothing? Look at the birds of the air: they neither sow nor reap nor gather into barns, and yet your heavenly Father feeds them. Are you not of more value than they? And which of you by being anxious can add a single hour to his span of life? And why are you anxious about

clothing? Consider the lilies of the field, how they grow: they neither toil nor spin, yet I tell you, even Solomon in all his glory was not arrayed like one of these. But if God so clothes the grass of the field, which today is alive and tomorrow is thrown into the oven, will he not much more clothe you, O you of little faith? Therefore do not be anxious, saying, "What shall we eat?" or "What shall we drink?" or "What shall we wear?" For the Gentiles seek after all these things, and your heavenly Father knows that you need them all. But seek first the kingdom of God and his righteousness, and all these things will be added to you. Therefore do not be anxious about tomorrow, for tomorrow will be anxious for itself. Sufficient for the day is its own trouble (Matt 6:25-34).

Jesus' command to not worry about what we will eat or drink comes immediately after a spiritual axiom He delivered in the preceding passage. "You cannot serve God and wealth," Jesus informs His disciples (Matt 6:24). "And *because* you cannot serve God and wealth," He continues, "I am going to tell you how to be free from the bondage of money: Do not be anxious about your life, what you will eat or what you will drink, nor about your body, what you will put on."

In other words, Jesus is telling His disciples to not consume their minds and hearts with concerns over having enough food or enough clothing. Why? Because God knows that His disciples need food and clothing and He is ready and able to provide His disciples with all their necessities. The birds of the sky and the flowers of the field are proof of God's faithful provision. God provides for the sparrow and He clothes the flowers of the field, yet His human creatures are infinitely more valuable than birds and lilies.

Jesus commands us to not worry about such things, because we have a heavenly Father who knows what we need and who has a reputation for lavishly providing for His creatures. Jesus' disciples, therefore, are meant to conclude that God will certainly provide them with everything they need. Armed with this knowledge, we can make the kingdom of God our chief pursuit rather than food and clothing.

But do those who have been freed by Jesus from the anxiety over food and clothing no longer possess capacities for earthly enjoyment? Not at all. Jesus did not say *do not eat food* (that was the strategy of the false teachers); rather, He says *do not be anxious about food*. Indeed, one of the greatest hindrances to enjoying God's good gifts in creation is to *worry* about whether or not we will have enough and what we will do if what we have gets taken away. It would seem, then, that those who trust God will be those who enjoy earthly life with greatest vigor. The removal of anxiety enhances the flavor of earthly pleasures. Seek first the kingdom of God (not food and drink), and earthly enjoyments will taste the way they were always intended to taste (see also Prov 24:13).

Now that we have considered Solomon's first exhortation and cleared away some objections that tend to arise in these kinds of discussions, let us now turn to chapter 3 and Solomon's command to celebrate life.

3

SOLOMON'S GREAT COMMISSION
CELEBRATE LIFE CONTINUALLY

*Let your garments be always white. Let not oil be
lacking on your head.*
Ecclesiastes 9:8

Solomon's first command is to savor life joyfully (Eccl
9:7). But he has more to say in this area of earthly
enjoyment. Moving from food and drink to physical
adornment, Solomon now exhorts us to live a life of
continual celebration. What will this look like? "Let your
garments be always white. Let not oil be lacking on your
head" (Eccl 9:8).

In Solomon's time, white clothing was used for
formal celebrations. Festal garments would usually be
white. But is the command here to literally always wear
white? While a few folks in the history of the church

took this as an absolute command, I don't think we are required to maintain a monochromatic wardrobe for two primary reasons.

First, nowhere else in the Old Testament does God mandate the color of one's clothing. In fact, the priests themselves would have been in violation of this principle due to the fact that they wore a multitude of colors (Exod 28). Second, nowhere in the New Testament does Scripture dictate one's color of clothing. In other words, neither the old or new covenant stipulations require faithful members of the covenant to perpetually adorn themselves in white apparel.

Rather, if we take the *reason* for why one would wear white clothing in the ancient Near East as our guiding hermeneutical principle, we can conclude that Solomon's command in this passage is for us to *live a celebratory life*. Clearly, Solomon is not ignoring the sorrows and the difficulties of life under the sun. He has considered these issues at length up to this point in Ecclesiastes, and he will continue to address these troubling realities in the latter sections of the book. Life in this fallen world is hard and full of sorrows, and Solomon is the first to recognize that. But for those who know the Creator and the Savior, earthly life should be characterized by celebration. Why? Because we know for certain that our life will end in celebration and eternity will be characterized by celebration.

Celebrating Now in Light of the Future

My wife is really good at celebrating life, and I believe she learned it from her mom. Amy will find any excuse to celebrate life—any excuse at all. We celebrate birthdays, and we celebrate half-birthdays because, well, why not? And because we have adopted our three children, we have the privilege of celebrating their individual "gotcha day"—the day we officially took them into our care and custody. We usually celebrate these days with donuts, and we sometimes celebrate other days with donuts—so we're eating a lot of donuts!

We celebrate holidays: Christmas, Easter, Thanksgiving, Mother's Day, Father's Day, Labor Day, Memorial Day, and Fourth of July. Due to our children's birth countries, we also celebrate Ethiopian Christmas and Chinese New Year. We also celebrate Cinco de Mayo, not because we've adopted from Mexico, but because we just want an excuse to eat some great Mexican food! We like to watch the Kentucky Derby or the Super Bowl and throw a party. We like to watch the NBA finals and watch Steph Curry drain some sweet threes! These are all gifts of God's goodness, and Christians are free to celebrate certain days or choose to refrain (Rom 14:5), but there is more to this kind of celebrating than just our present enjoyment of earthly life.

Like the enjoyment of food and wine, we celebrate in this life in anticipation of the ultimate wedding feast, a celebration that will include material pleasures. When you eat and you drink and celebrate life with other Christians in *this* life, you are experiencing a foretaste of a coming kingdom when we will be together with each other and our Bridegroom for the consummate wedding celebration. Consider John's description of this future event:

> Then I heard what seemed to be the voice of a great multitude, like the roar of many waters and like the sound of mighty peals of thunder, crying out,
>
>> "Hallelujah!
>> For the Lord our God
>> the Almighty reigns.
>> Let us rejoice and exult
>> and give him the glory,
>> for the marriage of the Lamb has come,
>> and his Bride has made herself ready;
>> it was granted her to clothe herself
>> with fine linen, bright and pure"—
>
> for the fine linen is the righteous deeds of the saints.
>
> And the angel said to me, "Write this: Blessed are those who are invited to the marriage supper of the Lamb." And he said to me, "These are the true words of God" (Rev 19:6-9).

The grand celebration of all history will be a royal wedding where the Bridegroom takes His bride to be His forever. This event calls for exuberant joy and praise to God, and it will be attended by a celebratory meal. But to spiritualize this marriage supper is to miss the entire drift of redemptive history. God created the physical universe and called it good (Gen 1:31), and He will re-create a physical universe and raise His people to a new bodily existence at the resurrection (Isa 65:17-25; John 5:29; Rev 21:1ff). There is no reason to believe that physical enjoyments of food and drink won't be part of this marriage celebration, or the existence of the new earth (see also Luke 14:15-24; Rev 22:2).

Yet, Instagram seems to tell us that there are plenty of people celebrating life these days, so we might wonder how Christian celebration is distinguished from the merriment of those who don't know Christ. First, we must understand that due to God's common grace, many people across the globe have the opportunity to enjoy the gift of earthly life whether or not they acknowledge the One who provides such earthly pleasures.[1] The pleasures of marriage, children, friendship, food, wholesome recreation, fulfilling work, and so on, are the gifts of a Creator who loves His enemies (Matt 5:44-49). While earthly blessing is no sign that one is right with God (Ps 46:16-20), such blessings are evidence of a good and gracious God whose kindness is meant to lead us to repentance (Rom 2:5).

Secondly, however, a Christian celebration of life is not pursued because these years on earth are our only chance at happiness—because "you only live once" (#YOLO). Rather, believers in Jesus Christ celebrate in this life because we know with certainty that when this earthly life ends, eternity begins, and continues in celebration! Like Solomon, the believer has come to realize that the ultimate satisfaction cannot be found in earthly pleasures. Such things, therefore, are not pursued as the primary aim of life. And, because of the resurrection, the believer doesn't fear when certain pleasures or opportunities for adventure and enjoyment are removed from him.

Bucket Lists, Resurrection, and the New Earth[2]

Earthly enjoyment, adventure, and celebration are pursued by many people as quickly-depleting commodities that must be consumed before their time on earth runs out. Often for people without an eternal perspective, life is structured and priorities are ordered in such a way to achieve as much pleasure in this life as possible. If you believe that this life is all there is and that upon death you simply pass out of conscious existence, it makes sense to do as much as you can before you die. Something like a "bucket list"—a catalog of items one hopes to accomplish before one dies—would become a primary concern because your opportunity to enjoy all the world has to offer may end upon your last heartbeat.

But how does a bucket list fit into the Christian worldview, especially as we consider the centrality of the resurrection in Scripture? One contemporary Christian author is concerned that believers are failing to live in light of the resurrection, and as a result, have taken on a "bucket list" mentality where the pursuit of earthly celebration and adventure becomes one of the primary purposes of their existence. This approach to life, however, doesn't square with what Scripture tells us about the age to come:

> [T]he "bucket list" mentality—that this life is our only chance to ever enjoy adventure and fun—flies in the face of the biblical teaching of the resurrection [see Is 26:19; Dan 12:2; 1 Cor 15:52-53; Phil 3:20-21]….Despite the centrality of the resurrection in Scripture and church history, many Christians have never been clearly taught its meaning, so they imagine they'll live forever in a disembodied state. In fact, of Americans who believe in a resurrection of the dead, two-thirds believe they will not have bodies after the resurrection.[3]

The ultimate Christian hope is not existence in a disembodied state; although to die and be with Christ at this moment would be gain (Phil 1:21). Even the apostle Paul who longed to be with the Lord looked forward to the resurrection, and sensed the incompleteness of his salvation without it (2 Cor 5:1-5; see also Phil 3:12-14). Why did the apostle long for the resurrection? Because at the resurrection we will receive new bodies in which we will worship and work and play on a new earth for all eternity. Even though most Christians won't be able to join any North Face expeditions in this life, thanks to God's gift of the resurrection we will never stop exploring.

The Scripture certainly doesn't prohibit us from making plans to enjoy certain things before we die. God is good, and He gives us all things richly to enjoy (1 Tim 6:17). But, as we've learned from Solomon, neither does Scripture encourage us to channel a bulk of our energy into fulfilling these kinds of desires nor to make such pursuits the main thing of life; to do so would be to hinder our enjoyment of God's gifts rather than enhance them.

The glory and grace of the resurrection and promise of a new earth is that it *frees* us to give our lives to serving Christ and serving others because we don't have to worry about really missing out on anything. There are a host of legitimate pleasures I would like enjoy before I die: bag a few serious peaks, ski the Swiss Alps, cycle across portions of Italy. I might get to complete one or more of these before I go to be with Jesus, or I might not. Ultimately, it doesn't matter. If it's for God's glory and my eternal happiness, God will make sure I experience it. If not on this earth, then in the new one to come.

When Solomon exhorts us to celebrate life, therefore, he is not suggesting that we pursue earthly enjoyment at the expense of sacrificial service to others (Phil 2:3-4). His words must be read within the context of the resurrection which, when rightly understood and integrated into our lives, actually delivers us from selfishness.

It is possible that the pursuit of something like a "bucket list" can easily take time and energy away from other priorities and encourage us to focus too much on ourselves. But if we are convinced that life on the new earth holds opportunity for unimaginable and unsurpassed enjoyment, we will be able to set aside our grand plans for global travel and adventure and give our lives to serving others. This approach to life may not get you a stunning collection of Instagram photos, but you will please your Master and bring joy to others. And that's better than 1,000 mountain-top selfies any day.

But only a Christian can live like this. Reader, if you are presently without Jesus Christ, the enjoyments of this life cannot provide you the satisfaction for which you are searching. Only Jesus Christ and His death on the cross for your sins can satisfy your soul (John 6:53). When your sins have been forgiven, you are enabled to behold this world as God's gift that you can enjoy without condemnation and you will taste this life the way it was meant to be tasted. But apart from Christ, you are only headed for eternal condemnation, *and the earthly pleasures you relish now will be as good as it ever gets for you.* On behalf of Christ, therefore, I urge you to be reconciled to God. Christ has died on the cross to pay the penalty for your sin and risen from the dead so that you can stand before God clothed in His perfect righteousness and freed from eternal condemnation.

Let Not Oil Be Lacking on Your Head

But celebration is just part of the command. "Let not oil be lacking on your head," Solomon tells us. But what could this mean? Like the previous statement, Solomon's words here are not to be taken as an absolute command.

The statement itself refers to fragrant oil in the ancient Near East that was used to soften and nourish the skin. Combined with the previous statement, Solomon is telling us to celebrate life by an appropriate care for our physical bodies and appearances. In the Bible, both wine and white clothing symbolize *joy*. One commentator puts it this way: "Don't wear sackcloth to work. Buy a white dress. Splash on a dash of cologne. Shampoo and rinse."[4]

True spirituality, contrary to what the false teachers were telling the church in Colossae, doesn't neglect the body or physical appearance. When a person purposefully disregards their physical appearance out of supposed devotion to God, they are actually expressing a false humility that is likely grounded in legalism and the attempt to earn God's favor through rejecting God's good gifts. Jesus said that if you fast, take care of your body in such a way so that no one knows that you are fasting (Matt 6:16-18).

Here's the stunning truth: The Christian who is free from the need to earn God's favor is free to rightly enjoy God's good gifts and caring for the body through clothing and cologne are some of those good gifts. One commentator puts it exceptionally well: "Ecclesiastes…does not advocate hedonism under the shadow of the gods ill-will, but contentment as part of God's gift, the outflow of an assurance of acceptance by him."[5] When we have peace with God we are enabled to rightly appropriate His gifts.

How Should Christians Care for their Physical Appearance?[6]

But Solomon's exhortation here brings us to ask the question of *how* Christians should care for their physical appearance. Biblically, we would be right to say that a Christian should neither neglect his or her physical appearance nor worship it. It is not a mark of holiness to allow your physical appearance to deteriorate through careless inattention, nor is it ultra-spiritual to purposefully neglect your clothing or hygiene. What, then, should mark our physical appearance? This is not an easy question to answer, for Scripture doesn't say too much on the subject. But I will attempt an answer that, I trust, makes reasonable use of what Scripture does say.

Intentionality in How We Dress – A Christian's life should be lived intentionally, not haphazardly (Prov 4:26; 21:5; Eccl. 9:10; Eph 5:15-17). This intentionality will often express itself in how we dress. A lack of intentionality in life is a mark of youth and immaturity, and a lack of intentionality in how we adorn ourselves may be an overflow of our life as a whole. Intentionality does not imply that we must wear expensive clothing or latest fashions (see 1 Pet 3:1ff), but only that we give some thought and attention to what we are wearing so as not to be a distraction to others. Even here, however, Christians will distinguish themselves by not giving undue attention to their clothing or fretting over how well their wardrobe matches the latest trends. The body is more than clothing, Jesus reminds us, so we don't need to consume ourselves with its adornment (Matt 6:25).

Adornment that's Fitting for the Occasion – Wearing what is appropriate for a given occasion is an expression of intentionality, and it shows respect for others (Matt 22:39; 1 Pet 2:13-14). If you wear pajamas to a formal gala, you will not only embarrass yourself, you will embarrass the host, the person who invited you, and make all the attendees feel awkward. This kind of neglect is a refusal to love one's neighbor as oneself.

Clothing That Doesn't Draw Attention for its Opulence or its Neglect – We should avoid distracting others with our wealth or drawing attention to ourselves by neglecting our physical appearance (1 Pet 3:1ff; Matt 6:16-18). In both cases—opulence and neglect—we are focused on ourselves rather than on Christ and others. If we are most concerned with drawing people's attention to Christ through our word, conduct, and character, then we will not be likely to dress in a such a way that draws undue attention to ourselves through our overly-fancy clothing or poor hygiene

Reasonable Care for Our Physical Health – Our physical health is a stewardship (Prov 20:29; 31:17; 1 Tim 4:8; 5:23). We should desire to remain useful to our King and to His people for as long as possible. Eating well (with self-control and a reasonable attention to healthy food), getting adequate sleep and exercise are ways we can steward our health. None of these guarantee that we will remain healthy, and some of us may suffer illnesses that hinder our ability to exercise and make it difficult to maintain our weight. Nor do these principles imply that we won't ever be called to endanger our health for others. Love for others may require that kind of sacrifice, and Jesus and Paul are our example (Luke 9:44, 51; Acts 20:24). But for our part, we should desire to maintain our health so we can labor diligently for the Lord and for others as long as possible.

Attention to Our Personal Hygiene – Personal hygiene is a matter of *loving one's neighbor* (Song 7:8; Matt 22:39). Poor physical hygiene makes others around us uncomfortable. Brush your teeth. Take a shower. Comb your hair. Wear deodorant. Chew gum when necessary. Personal hygiene is not primarily about you; it's about respect for others.

In every way we care for our physical appearance, we must always make humility our most important piece of apparel (1 Pet 5:5). In all we do we are to glorify God and consider others as more important than ourselves (1 Cor 10:31; Phil 2:3), and this focus on God's glory and our neighbor's good will guide us, even in how we adorn ourselves.

Conclusion

Solomon's exhortations in this section should lead us to conclude that the physical world matters. Yes, our material existence is marred by a fall, and sin easily tempts us to misuse and misappropriate God's gifts. But as we learned in this chapter, both the resurrection of Jesus Christ and the hope of our future resurrection provide indisputable proof that God values the material world. By God's grace Christians have the capacity to rightly understand the place that earthly enjoyment is meant to have in this life because they are able to see, by faith, into a future where the celebration never ends. We are able to adorn our bodies with clothing that both beautifies and avoids the vanity. In the next chapter we will consider Solomon's command to enjoy life thankfully.

4

SOLOMON'S GREAT COMMISSION
ENJOY LIFE THANKFULLY

*Enjoy life with the wife whom you love, all the days of your
fleeting life that he has given you under the sun, because that is
your portion in life and in your toil at which
you toil under the sun.*
Ecclesiastes 9:9

In the previous two chapters we've reflected upon
Solomon's commands to enjoy God's gifts of eating and
drinking and his call to cultivate a celebratory life with a
heavenward focus. In the verse we are pondering in this
chapter, Solomon continues with this theme to enjoy
life, but he now broadens out his application beyond
food and drink to *all of life*.

A World of Pleasure

Not only has God given us food to eat, He has given us thousands of legitimate pleasures to enjoy in this life. A walk in a wooded park on a warm summer's evening, a long conversation with a friend, a good book, a new dress, a warm cup of tea on a chilly winter morning, a meal with your family and friends on your back patio, a long bike ride through the countryside, the gentle nuzzling of a newborn baby, the aroma of a fresh bag of coffee beans, sunflower seeds at a baseball game with your son. There are a multitude of good, wholesome, God-approved and God-given enjoyments that Christians can gladly receive from their heavenly Father (James 1:17).

This brief list of innocent earthly enjoyments demonstrates that life is infused at every turn with pleasure. For those who have eyes to see, these little pleasures are glimpses of God's own happiness and goodness (Ps 19:1-2; Acts 14:26; 1 Tim 1:11). When we turn from the things of this world as the chief source of meaning and satisfaction, to Christ as Lord and Savior and the fountain of all delights (Ps 16:11), we aren't drawn away from these earthly pleasures; rather, our eyes are opened to behold the glory and goodness of God *in* these earthly pleasures as we enjoy them the way they were intended to be enjoyed: not as that which provide ultimate satisfaction, but as gifts meant to offer some temporary satisfaction.

The Gift of Companionship

But Solomon doesn't only tell us to enjoy life; he tells us to "enjoy life with the wife whom you love." In other words, don't enjoy life alone; enjoy it with your God-given, life-long companion. Your wife is your friend, and she is God's gift to you (Prov 18:22; 31:10). Marriage was designed by our Creator to be a source of tremendous blessing to His earthly creatures (Gen 2:22-25), and Solomon exhorts his readers to receive this gift with joy and thanksgiving.

Notice, however, that Solomon says to enjoy life *with* your wife, not enjoy *your wife*. Solomon certainly isn't denigrating the pleasure of sexual intimacy within marriage. The joys of pure sexual intimacy are included in Solomon's statement to "enjoy life with the wife." Solomon wrote the Song of Solomon, which is a glorious and tasteful celebration of the exquisite pleasures of marital intimacy. He also wrote Proverbs 5:16-19, which speaks rather straightforwardly on the same theme. The blessings of sexual intimacy are to be enjoyed by married couples with exuberance and heart-felt thankfulness to God.

Yet, while not disregarding the blessings of marital sexual intimacy, Solomon is here emphasizing the blessings of marital *companionship*. The command in this text is to embrace this life and its enjoyments, not by yourself, but with your spouse. Over the decades, as couples weather trials and traverse a multitude of experiences together, they come to value most highly the friendship of their spouse. At least this should be the case. Some of us, sadly, will look back over our lives and recognize that we allowed other ambitions to crowd out the simple pleasure of enjoying life with our spouse. Some of us need to hear these words from David Gibson:

> If you are too busy to enjoy the life you have together, then you are too busy. End of story. If you do not enjoy each other, then it is likely that you are simply taking what you can from each other to pursue other goals and ambitions that are never going to give you all they promise. You may use each other to gain something that will turn out not to be gain—and lose each other in the process.[1]

For many couples, Christians included, the relationship that once began with intense affection for one another is now just sputtering along, maintained primarily for its usefulness to get what the other spouse wants out of life and because divorce is too inconvenient. Years of stress at work, family pressures, and neglect have conspired to rob the relationship of the joy, playfulness, and friendship that once characterized the marriage. It is no wonder why Solomon must command his listeners to enjoy life with their spouse. Some of us need to be re-awakened to the gift we've been given in our spouse and to steward it well during our short time on earth.

Stewardship in this case refers to our responsibility to enjoy this life with our companion and to rekindle our marital friendship.

All of Your Life

Solomon's exhortation to enjoy life with our spouse is a command that does not expire until the end of this life. You are to enjoy life with your spouse "all the days of your fleeting life that he has given you under the sun." The word "fleeting" is the word translated "vain" elsewhere in Ecclesiastes (e.g., 1:2; 1:14; 2:1) and is translated here as "vain" by the *English Standard Version*. It is best understood here, not as "vain, useless," or "pointless," but "brief, momentary," and "passing." Solomon's point is that this earthly life is short, full of constant toil, and beset with trouble. But you must, nevertheless, receive your marriage as a good gift from God. The earthly gift of marriage is "your portion in life and in your toil at which you toil under the sun." Yes, life is hard and often monotonous, but God has given you a companion designed specifically for your happiness with whom you can enjoy life.

It's true that marriage between men and women is *only* for this life and that in the new heavens and new earth, there will be no more individual marriages because we will be married corporately to Jesus Christ as His bride (Mark 12:25; cf. Eph 5:22-33; Rev 19:6-8). It is also true that in light of Christ's first coming and the inauguration of the latter days, singleness takes on a new meaning that it previously did not have. Singleness is now a gift (*charismata*) that is to be used to benefit the people of God (1 Cor 12:7). That is, those who have the gift of singleness have been endowed with a special capacity to serve Christ's church without the distractions of a spouse and children (1 Cor 7:25-35).

This gift of singleness, however, is relatively rare, and Paul still sees marriage as the normal state for most people, including Christians (1 Cor 7:1-5). If you are married, therefore, Solomon's exhortation is to renew your joy in your wife and to enjoy life together with her. Indeed, like we saw earlier in chapter 2, Solomon commands the enjoyment of legitimate earthly pleasures as one of the means by which we endure life in a fallen world with all its difficulties, enigmas, and unpredictability.

Marriage, while attended with its own difficulties (see 1 Cor 7:32-34), is one of those lawful gifts that God provides His people so that they might navigate this life with joy and perseverance. That's why Solomon reminds us that the companionship of marriage is "your portion in life and in your toil at which you toil under the sun" (Eccl 9:9). Life is hard and full of toil. The answer to this difficulty? Get married and enjoy life with your bride. If you are married, let Solomon's exhortations reorient your affections and priorities, and receive this good gift with thankfulness.

With Thankfulness

The exhortation in this verse is to enjoy life *thankfully*. While the command to be thankful is not explicit in this text, it is implicit in the way Solomon reminds his readers that marriage is a temporary gift that God has provided for His creatures for their joy. Given the temporary nature of this gift and the aim for which God gave it, it would be unfitting to not continually thank God for it. Besides, Solomon has expanded his exhortation to include all of life, so now every legitimate pleasure we taste in this life is an opportunity to thank God.

I wonder, however, how often we neglect the basic discipline of thankfulness? While I don't think we need to bow our heads in prayer at every chocolate chip cookie or autumn sunset, our hearts should be regularly thanking God for His goodness to us, even in the little things. Thankfulness, according to the apostle Paul, is characteristic of a Christian's life (Col 3:15-17; 1 Thess 5:18). But perhaps we aren't as thankful as we should be because we are too lazy to enjoy life.

Too Lazy to Enjoy Life?

We've already noted that Solomon is not making suggestions at this point in his book: he is *commanding* us to savor, celebrate, and enjoy life. Given our sinfulness, however, it should come as no surprise that it is necessary to command God's people to enjoy life.

I am reminded of a time while I was discipling a young man when he admitted to me that he rarely ate breakfast during the winter months because it was too cold to make the brief walk from his apartment to the student union. Failing to eat a reasonable breakfast was having other negative effects in his life, yet he was unwilling to bundle up, brave the cold, and sit himself in front of a warm morning meal. He needed a gentle yet firm admonishment to shun laziness, even in an area that didn't appear to require much attention.

But lest we are too hard on this young man, consider the times that you refused to grab a cup of coffee, make your favorite meal, or take a refreshing hike because to do so would be, from your perspective, too difficult. I remember a time when, shortly after being married, I was watching a movie while eating chips and salsa. My salsa supply was soon depleted but I still had a few more chips. Walking all twenty feet to the refrigerator, however, was simply out of the question. Rather than finish my snack in a way that would have brought more pleasure, I chose, rather, to forego the salsa and just eat the chips. I could multiply examples. I'm sure you could, too.

You might be surprised that Scripture actually addresses this issue of laziness in pursuing legitimate pleasures. The Proverbs have many unflattering things to say about the sluggard, and this may be one of the least complimentary:

"Whoever is slothful will not roast his game,
but the diligent man will get precious wealth"
(12:27).

"The sluggard buries his hand in the dish,
and will not even bring it back to his mouth"
(19:24).

The sluggard in Scripture is the one who refuses to
work, maintain his home and livelihood, and, as it turns
out, one who doesn't even exert himself to attain God-
given enjoyments. The sluggard had the wherewithal to
kill his game, but he was willing to settle for uncooked
food rather than roast it.[2] He had the capacity to make
a move to feeding himself and put his hand in the dish,
but actually tasting the food was just too hard of a task.

In His wisdom, God has given us commands to
rouse us from our spiritual apathy and indifference.
Occasionally we need reminders to enjoy life the way
God intends for us to enjoy it: with our marital
companions and with serious effort.

What About Suffering?
But as we again broach the topic of enjoying life, we
must ask a question we posed earlier: where does
suffering fit in the discussion? We've noted Solomon's
unflinching gaze into life's painful realities—he is no
stranger to suffering. We've also observed that life's
lawful enjoyments are one of the means God has given

us to persevere through suffering. Indeed, sometimes life's simple pleasures are enhanced during times of trial.

I was reminded of this reality during my time in seminary. A good friend of mine had come into a severe trial. He had been slandered in an unimaginable way, and he was now facing serious legal trouble due to the false charges. At the peak of this trial, my friend never blamed God, and he continued to worship, pray, care for his family, and work hard. He was an example of true godliness in the midst of suffering.

During this time my friend said something to me one day while we were at work together that I'll never forget. While eating some pasta-salad during our lunch break, he said that he had noticed that the little things of life—his wife's pasta-salad, for example—seemed to provide him fresh enjoyment while under the affliction of a severe trial. While suffering, he came to appreciate even more God's kindness to him in providing him a tasty lunch. As one author has noted, "Times of sorrow can tenderize us to appreciate little, everyday, otherwise forgettable blessings."[3] This is one of the ways God enables us to thank Him in all circumstances (1 Thess 5:18). Christians don't drown their sorrows in earthly pleasure as though they can provide ultimate healing and escape, but we do receive such gifts as God's grace and thank Him for them.

Conclusion

It shouldn't surprise us that Solomon must exhort us to enjoy life with our spouse. As we've already noted, Solomon derives his outlook on life from a solid theology of creation, and one of the main features of creation was God's formation of man and woman created in His image for the sake of marital companionship (Gen 2:24). Nor should it surprise us that Solomon widens his scope to include an exhortation to enjoy all of life. While Solomon doesn't ignore the realities of suffering, he doesn't allow those realities to dampen the joy that God's people were intended to have during their earthly life. Indeed, sometimes our trials sweeten the smallest of life's pleasures and enable us to experience the goodness of God, even when we may be presently feeling the effects of the Fall in our suffering.

But Solomon isn't done with us, yet. He has one more command we must reckon with. It is to this command that we turn in the following chapter.

5

SOLOMON'S GREAT COMMISSION
LIVE LIFE INTENTIONALLY

Whatever your hand finds to do, do it with your might, for there is no work or thought or knowledge or wisdom in Sheol, to which you are going.
Ecclesiastes 9:10

In the previous chapters Solomon has boldly challenged us to savor life, celebrate life, and enjoy life with our spouse. In this last verse, Solomon will turn our attention to one more source of legitimate earthly satisfaction: work.

Yes, work.

Some of us might be a little less enthused about this particular exhortation than we were about the previous three. For some Christians, work is a drudgery: an intrusive yet necessary burden to bear on the way to our eternal rest. An exhortation to work, therefore, doesn't sound nearly as attractive as the call to enjoy life's good pleasures. But what if work is one of life's good pleasures?

The reason why some of us bristle at the suggestion that work is one of life's pleasures is because we have never thoroughly understood what Scripture teaches about work. While this is not the place to provide a full biblical theology of work, we can, with Solomon, go again back to Genesis one more time to hear where he has developed his view on work.

Solomon's exhortation in Ecclesiastes 9:10 is built upon a theology of work that God had established early in the creation narrative. Immediately after God created Adam, He placed him in the garden to "work it and keep it" (Gen 2:15). There are two observations in this text that are vital to Solomon's exhortation in Ecclesiastes 9:10.

First, Adam's assignment to work and keep the garden was given *prior* to the Fall, not after it. This chronological sequence is significant because it grounds work as an essential component of creation, not an aberration that appeared after the entrance of sin into the world. By the way they talk about work, it seems as though some Christians think work was a task that became necessary after the Fall that interrupted what was an otherwise leisurely and work-free existence for

God's image bearers. In other words, some think work is a result of the Fall, not the express intention of creation.

It is not difficult to see how such a view of work would inhibit one's joy in their work. If work is not something essential to creation but is, rather, a result of sin's entrance into the world, then the best I can do is bear this burden until I get to heaven when I can finally put an end to my labor and toil.

The biblical narrative, however, teaches us that God's original intention in forming humans was that they would engage in productive labor by exercising dominion over the entire earth (Gen 1:26-31). Work, therefore, is fundamental to our very personhood as God's image bearers. Indeed, as God's little images, we are to imitate our Creator who fashioned this grand universe with the skill of a wise craftsman (see Ps 19:1-2; Prov 8:22-31). Individually, God gave us minds and bodies with the capacity to accomplish significant tasks of building, designing, researching, discovering, and planning. Corporately, we were created for mutual interdependence where we labor according to our God-given gifts and skills in order to serve and provide for each other.

The Fall, therefore, did not create an environment in which work was now *necessary*; rather, it created an environment where work was now *frustrated*. Due to God's curse upon the earth, the woman's calling to bear and raise children and help her husband would be beset with physical pain and relational turmoil (Gen 3:16). The man's calling to bring forth sustenance from the ground would be hindered by difficulty and occasional futility (Gen 3:17-19). The curse, however, did not make that which was created good (Gen 1:31) now inherently bad. Rather, the Fall and its subsequent fallout made that which was inherently good liable to inherent difficulty, misuse, and neglect.

The second observation we need to make in connection with Solomon's plea in Ecclesiastes 9:10 is that the word translated "work" here is used elsewhere in the Old Testament to refer to religious service in general and serving the Lord in particular (see Deut 11:13; 28:14; Josh 22:5). The work Adam was to perform was productive labor—the maintenance, development, and protection of the garden—yet this work was viewed as service to God. In other words, Adam's labor to tend the garden, guard it from intruders, and exercise dominion over his little plot of land was, in and of itself, spiritual work unto God. This is an important point because some of us may tend to think about our work (whether it is a career in finance or caring for a home and children) as inherently less pleasing or valuable to God than what we might call "church work." Genesis 2:15 teaches us, however, that our daily work itself *is* service to God and no less important than the work in which we might engage at church.

Do it with Your Might!

So how do believers, now equipped with a robust doctrine of creation, approach their daily lives? With zest. With intentionality. With Spirit-filled vigor. "Whatever your hand finds to do," Solomon commands, "do it with your might." Do you hear the intensity and urgency in Solomon's words? He is crying out to those who know the Creator and saying, "Don't coast through life! Work hard. Stop meandering through each day, aimless and half-hearted. Work! Be productive! Produce things of value for other people. Accomplish something! And put your heart and energy into it, whatever it might be."

Why must we hear this exhortation as Christians? Because in Christ we are *finally alive*. Every facet of our being is now infused with new spiritual energy (Col 1:29), and this new energy should express itself in a zest for earthly life, especially in being productive with work that blesses others. "Religion," as one Christian writer has said, "does not take a man away from his work; it sends him into his work with an added quality of devotion."[1]

Like his discovery of pleasure and wisdom's inherent limitations, Solomon also realized that work and productivity couldn't ultimately satisfy his soul. Once he recognized this, however, he was able to see the place that work did have in the realm of human satisfaction and contentment. We were designed by God to find joy in our work and in productive labor.

We are to reflect our Creator who, after a full work-week, stepped back from His grand project and said, "That's very good" (Gen 1:31). Men and women are made in the image of God and created to work, exercise dominion, produce, create, to bring order out of chaos, and to reflect the person of God by planning and building and fashioning and nurturing and instructing the next generation.

It is no wonder, then, Solomon also penned several Proverbs that exalt diligence and chide laziness. The person who is diligent in their work will receive material and spiritual wealth (Prov 10:4; 13:4; 21:5), find themselves in places of leadership (Prov 12:24), and enjoy high-level recognition for their skillful labor (Prov 22:29). Those who live intentionally and work hard in all their endeavors will often taste the satisfaction of success while avoiding the needless difficulties that attend laziness (Prov 15:19; 20:30). The sluggard, however, will mainly experience physical and spiritual poverty (Prov 10:4; 13:4; 20:4; 21:25) and rarely attain to any level of prominence (Prov 12:24). The only recognition the sluggard will receive from their employer is disappointment and an eventual pink slip (Prov 10:26).

The reason Scripture speaks so strongly about these twin issues of diligence and laziness is because God created us for the very purpose of exercising dominion over this earth He has created—a calling that requires persistent labor (Gen 1:28). To neglect this calling as God's image-bearers is to disregard a fundamental aspect of our personhood. When we yield to the temptation of laziness, we never find the hardy satisfaction we expected to find because we are acting contrary to the way we were made. It is not unusual for those who are not presently working (due to their own choice or some unavoidable circumstances) to more easily succumb to depression.[2]

On the other hand, as William Barrick observes, "Work forms a significant aspect of God-given joys."[3] In his classic book on work, *The Religious Tradesman*, Richard Steele challenges us to test this truth against our own experience: "I dare appeal to every one's experience, whether they find not more inward peace and satisfaction when the day has been diligently employed in their proper callings, than when it has been trifled away in sloth and folly."[4] We all know that acquiescing to the lure of laziness never satisfies our souls the way that careful, diligent, determined work does.

None of this is meant to suggest that work will be pleasurable all of the time. As we noted above, the Fall introduced futility into the world while also tainting our attitude toward work. Work is still a good gift, but it will sometimes be frustrating, fruitless, and seemingly pointless. Occasionally we will labor diligently on a project or assignment, only to see our productivity evaporate due to an equipment failure, computer crash, or budgetary decisions made by those in management.

We will be tempted by apathy, laziness, or a general lack of motivation. The job you currently have may be unusually difficult and you might be underpaid for a season.

Nevertheless, Solomon, following what God revealed about the creation in the Genesis narrative, reminds us that work is a divine gift from which we can (and should!) derive satisfaction. Indeed, understanding how God has made us to work will enable us to persevere through these times of futility and frustration to make the most of our present situation. While there are plenty of legitimate reasons for seeking a new job or line of work, it is important to remember that switching jobs may not be the answer to your present discontent.

What About Prolonged Seasons of Dissatisfaction at Work?[5]

It's possible that some of your dissatisfaction is a direct result of the curse. Futility and frustration will creep into the best of jobs, and you may be simply experiencing some unpleasant features of life in a fallen world. But there is another possibility. It could be that you are attempting to locate your satisfaction primarily in the work itself rather than in faithfulness to your Master.

It's true that God has given man work as a gift and, like God, we can derive an immense amount of joy and fulfillment from it. But it's also true that our *ultimate* hope for satisfaction cannot reside in the work itself, for there may be times when we are faced with tasks that we do not find immediately compelling or fulfilling. From where will our joy come at these times? The Scripture draws us to a place where satisfaction is steady and reliable. Consider Paul's counsel in Ephesians 6:5-8:

> Bondservants, obey your earthly masters with fear and trembling, with a sincere heart, as you would Christ, not by the way of eye-service, as people-pleasers, but as bond-servants of Christ, doing the will of God from the heart, rendering service with a good will as to the Lord and not to man, knowing that whatever good anyone does, this he will receive back from the Lord, whether he is a bondservant or is free.

Where do we ground our joy as we work? In faithfulness to Christ. We are to obey our employers (our "earthly masters") as we would Christ, not for the sake of recognition, but as a way of serving God. Note that Paul links "obeying our earthly masters" to "doing the will of God." When we complete the work we've been given by those in authority over us, we are actually doing God's will! If you wonder what God's will is for you during your work day, think first about the tasks *you've been given* by your employer and seek diligently to complete those responsibilities. Drawing from Richard Steele's wisdom once again, this kind of approach to work "will ennoble the meanest employment, and secure your highest end and truest happiness, whatever your success be in other respects."[6]

It is important to note that this passage about how we should serve our earthly masters is given in a book in which Paul has already discussed the topic of good works. Earlier in the letter, Paul tells his readers that they were saved by grace apart from works for the express purpose of doing good works (Eph 2:8-10; see also Titus 2:14). But these good works are not hidden or difficult to identify, nor do they need to be invented or devised by our imagination. Rather, God has already planned and prepared the works that Christians are meant to fulfill: "For we are his workmanship, created in Christ Jesus for good works, which God prepared beforehand that we should walk in them" (Eph 2:10).

The same word used for "good" (*agathos*) in Paul's passage about how we should conduct ourselves in the workplace is the same word for "good" used in Ephesians 2:10. The Lord will bless us according to "whatever good" we've done in the workplace in submission to our earthly master out of reverence to Christ (Eph 6:8). Given the reality that God has made us to work and, by His good providence, located us in our present place of employment, it is reasonable to conclude that our daily occupation is one of the primary areas in which God has prepared for us to walk in good works (see also 1 Cor 7:17).[7]

A Steady Source of Satisfaction

As we approach our work in the way Paul describes above, we will find a steady source of satisfaction, even if we are in a job that we hope is not permanent. It may seem counter-intuitive, but on the days that we mostly pursue the things we *want* to do rather than the things we know we *should* do (out of boredom, lack of motivation, an incessant need for diversion, or just plain laziness), we are often left with far less satisfaction than when we simply fulfill our obvious obligations.

None of this is meant to suggest that a Christian should never look for a job in which they are more interested or for which they are more qualified. But we must keep in mind that jumping from one job to another will never finally settle the satisfaction issue. There will be thorns and thistles in the most pleasant of fields, so we need to find a more consistent, stable source of fulfillment. When we prioritize our day according to those things we know we should do and we do them for the glory of God and the benefit of our neighbor, we can have confidence that we are exercising faithfulness to Christ. And faithfulness will lead to satisfaction in God and satisfaction in our work.

So, Solomon's command for you is to take work seriously, *whatever it is*. Whether you are a financial consultant or a mother of two, a computer programmer or a plumber; whether you are drawing up blueprints for a building or preparing a meal for your family; whether you are operating on a blocked artery or cleaning and managing your busy home; whether you are lifting weights or installing new sod in your front yard; whether you are painting the bathroom or trimming the hedges; whether you are running your own business or planning a weekend trip for you and your husband; whether you are preparing a sermon or setting up chairs for a fellowship meal; whether you are sharing the gospel or sharing your money, writing a blog post, a book, or an email, the point is this: live with intentionality and zest. Exercise diligence. Be intentional. Be productive for the good of others and the glory of God (see Col 3:23). In Christ there is legitimate satisfaction to be found in hard work and purposeful living, and Solomon exhorts you to find it.

Whatever Your Hand Finds to Do

It is important that we give attention to the sentence, "Whatever your hand finds to do." Solomon is not merely exhorting us to work hard at our job, as important as that is for the Christian (see Eph 6:5-9; 2 Thess 3:6-12). That is why I have avoided the term "work-ethic" so far in our discussion. Because this phrase usually bears connotations that relate exclusively to one's career, I think it is better to maintain the use of the word "diligence." Biblically, we are called to exercise diligence in *every* area of our lives, not just the area in which we earn an income. There are many people who have been wildly successful in their careers whose marriages have fallen into chaos because they were not diligent to nurture their relationship with their spouse. We might be tempted to look at their lives and admire their so-called work-ethic and all they were able to accomplish. The truth is that, despite their success, these people were actually sluggards in important portions of their life. Solomon's call to us is to live with our might in *all* that God has placed before us, not just a few select areas.

But what is the reason we should live with such vigor? Notice the following sentence: "For there is no work or thought or wisdom or knowledge in Sheol, to which you are going." The reason why we are to make the most of our time on earth is because life is short and we will soon die.

Now, you might think that's a dour note to end on. It sounds like Solomon is merely saying, "Life is short, you'll die, so work hard." But how is that encouraging? Well, in answering this question we must understand that Solomon is not rejecting the afterlife as though he is saying, "This is the only chance you get to work, so make the most of it." Due to his biblical view of creation, Solomon knows that work is not something that will be discarded as we transition to eternity (see also Rev 7:15). Solomon knows there is an afterlife to which believers are to look forward. He's hinted at it already in this book, and he will affirm the reality of an afterlife in Ecclesiastes 11 and 12. There is a judgment and an afterlife.

In this text, however, Solomon is speaking strictly in terms of earthly life under the sun. There is coming a day when we will no longer be able to work and plan and think about this life. The point, then, is to make the most of this gift of earthly life while you are still on this earth. Live life purposefully. There is only a short amount of time that you have here on earth, so make the most of it for the glory of Jesus Christ and for the benefit of others (Eph 5:15-17).

Conclusion

Earthly life is a gift, and work is a significant part of this gift. The calling to work and exercise dominion over this earth is fundamental to who we are as humans. When we neglect to work, we often suffer from depression, aimlessness, spiritual frustration, and, eventually, financial trouble. While the world may view work either as a means to acquire wealth and status or as a drudgery to endure until retirement, Scripture portrays work as one of the primary ways we glorify God with our lives. God made us and outfitted us with physical bodies and minds so that we might work to bless others and find satisfaction in a job well done. Solomon helpfully reminds us that our work should be attended with intentionality, vigor and joy.

Now that we've examined Solomon's four-fold exhortation to enjoy life, we now turn in the final chapter to answer some important questions so that we might apply these truths more deeply to our lives.

6

A THEOLOGY OF EARTHLY LIFE

As we come to the final chapter, let me ask you: have you been slightly unnerved by Solomon's boldness in the last four verses we examined? Have you found yourself a little uncomfortable with his unabashed and unqualified call to savor life joyfully (chapter 2), celebrate life continually (chapter 3), enjoy life thankfully (chapter 4), and live life purposefully (chapter 5)? Are you still uneasy at the prospect of heeding such commands? Perhaps you are afraid of losing sight of Jesus Christ and spiritual realities by enjoying life a little too much?

The Call for Self-Denial

This is a legitimate concern. Jesus warns us that it is possible for "the cares of the world and the deceitfulness of riches and the desires for other things

[to] enter in and choke the word," so that in the end the word "proves unfruitful" in the heart and life of the professing believer (Mark 4:18-19). In other words, there is a way of enjoying earthly life that actually imperils your soul. Additionally, Jesus calls His disciples to deny themselves and even *hate* their own lives in order to save their souls into eternity:

> And he said to all, "If anyone would come after me, let him deny himself and take up his cross daily and follow me. For whoever would save his life will lose it, but whoever loses his life for my sake will save it. For what does it profit a man if he gains the whole world and loses or forfeits himself? For whoever is ashamed of me and of my words, of him will the Son of Man be ashamed when he comes in his glory and the glory of the Father and of the holy angels. But I tell you truly, there are some standing here who will not taste death until they see the kingdom of God" (Luke 9:23-27).

> If anyone comes to me and does not hate his own father and mother and wife and children and brothers and sisters, yes, and even his own life, he cannot be my disciple (Luke 14:26).

The requirement is that Christ's disciples give up *everything* for the sake of following Him. "So therefore, any one of you who does not renounce all that he has cannot be my disciple" (Luke 14:33). What do these texts mean, and how do they square with Solomon's exhortations to enjoy earthly life?

We must give full voice to Jesus' words in the Gospels. These are calls to basic discipleship, not to next-level discipleship. That is, Jesus' radical statements about what it takes to follow Him are given to *all* who would make a profession to know Him. If we want to be saved, we must come to Christ and be willing to lose our earthly life and all that it provides in order to attain the life to come. If we are not willing to bear suffering and loss in this life for the glory of Christ and the sake of our eternal souls, then we are not yet ready to be Christ's disciples; we are not yet Christians.

This is what it means to deny oneself. Jesus isn't talking primarily about denying ourselves legitimate pleasures—like a cookie after dinner—but about a wholesale approach to earthly life where we value Him over everything else earthly life offers. In the context of Luke 9:23-27, Jesus is speaking about denying our natural tendency to protect ourselves and to guard what brings us pleasure and comfort when these things are in danger. That is why Jesus connects self-denial with the warning of what will happen if we are characterized by being ashamed of Christ in this life. We naturally desire to be well-liked and safe, so when our earthly life and possessions and reputation are threatened by our profession of faith, our natural tendency is to retreat from our position and to be ashamed of Christ. When someone is characterized by this reluctance to confess Christ publicly on earth, Jesus says they can have no assurance that He will confess them publicly at the final judgment. In other words, those who are constantly ashamed of Christ can have no assurance that they are going to heaven.

But when someone does give up everything and comes to Christ, they shed their former commitment to this world as the source of ultimate satisfaction, meaning, and pleasure; earthly enjoyments and high regard from the world are no longer our primary aims in life. Solomon teaches us that when this conversion occurs, the believer is finally able to enjoy earthly life in the way it was intended and according to right proportions. When Christ is *the* supreme joy of our lives (Ps 43:4), that which He has created becomes one of the means by which we taste and see that the Lord is good (Ps 34:8), not the idol with which we replace Him. That which we are no longer clutching for ultimate safety and fulfillment becomes a source of sweet—albeit temporary—satisfaction.

Jesus' warning in the parable of the soils helps believers maintain a Christ-ward focus during our life on this earth so that no earthly enjoyment outstrips our love for and obedience to our Savior. The warning in Mark 4:18-19 acts as a guardrail on the path of our obedience to Ecclesiastes 9:7-10. We endanger our souls and dilute the taste of earthly pleasure when we make earthly pleasure the chief pursuit of our lives. But when Christ satisfies our spiritual palate, that which He provides us in this life satisfies our physical palate. "The righteous has enough to satisfy his appetite, but the belly of the wicked suffers want" (Prov 14:25).

The Danger of Self-Denial

But some of us will guard against this tendency to drift from Christ by attempting to avoid earthly pleasures through self-denial. Instead of letting earthly pleasures skew you off course, you simply reject them altogether, or at least you try to. It is true that although some things are lawful, as the apostle Paul observes, not all things are helpful (1 Cor 10:23). Therefore, a Christian who has an alcoholic past may wisely set aside alcohol while recognizing it is fine for others to drink. Someone who is prone to watch too much television may need to put the T.V. away for a while. Things that are not necessarily wrong in and of themselves may be a stumbling block for some people.

On the whole, however, the Bible doesn't have us approach the good things of life this way. In fact, the New Testament warns us about false spirituality that says, "do not handle, do not taste, and do not touch" (Col 2:21). Rather, Scripture would have us receive these good gifts with thankfulness and joy. This passage in Ecclesiastes and this discussion about earthly pleasure is not merely about enjoying God's good gifts; it's about what constitutes genuine spirituality.

The Doctrine of Demons?

What if I told you that a few days ago I overheard a professing Christian propounding some Satanic teaching? To what kind of doctrine do you think I was referring? Might you think I was referring to someone teaching that God doesn't know the future, or that Jesus didn't rise from the dead, or that Scripture contains formal errors and contradictions? All of these are false doctrines that have their origin in the father of lies (John 8:44), but there is a kind of teaching that the apostle Paul calls demonic that may actually surprise us.

How about this statement: "God would be more pleased with you if you remained single," or "It's more spiritual to eat only vegetables and not meat." Paul actually calls this kind of teaching, not foolish or mistaken or misguided, but demonic. Although they may seem innocent enough, these prohibitions are actually from the pit of hell.

> Now the Spirit expressly says that in later times some will depart from the faith by devoting themselves to deceitful spirits and teachings of demons, through the insincerity of liars whose consciences are seared, who forbid marriage and require abstinence from foods that God created to be received with thanksgiving by those who believe and know

the truth. For everything created by God is good, and nothing is to be rejected if it is received with thanksgiving, for it is made holy by the word of God and prayer (1 Tim 4:1-5).

Why does Paul have such strong words for these seemingly innocuous statements? Because they reject the goodness of God and deny God His rightful glory for providing such gifts to His creatures. God created food and marriage for our joy so that we would, *in* the enjoyment itself, turn to God and say, "Thank you, Father, for such wonderful, kind, and gracious gifts. You are good and your steadfast love endures forever" (1 Tim 4:4-5; see Ps 100:5)!

These teachings are also Satanic because they implicitly deny the gospel of Jesus Christ. Christ came to be our all-sufficient Savior and to provide us with *everything we need* for salvation: Perfect righteousness and right standing with God, full payment for our sins, resurrection, and the gift of the Spirit to help us kill remaining sin in our lives. Whenever someone rejects, for religious reasons, earthly pleasures that God has ordained by His Word for His creatures' happiness, they do so due to a deficient understanding of the gospel. They are attempting to supplement Christ's work with their asceticism and thus rob the Savior of His glory, veil the gospel with human works, and confuse both believers and unbelievers. Demonic.

Enjoying Life and Keeping a Good Conscience

Paul concludes his discussion of demonic doctrines by affirming that "everything God has created is good and nothing is to be rejected if it is received with thanksgiving." This statement is not only a helpful affirmation of legitimate earthly pleasure, it also provides us with a test of how we are presently receiving earthly enjoyments. Ask yourself: can you receive such and such earthly gift—whatever it might be—from God with *thanksgiving*? Are you regularly thanking God for the pleasures in which you partake in this life? One commentator puts it like this:

> [Paul's comments in 1 Tim 4:1-5] giv[e] us a good test to use for all our earthly pleasures. When I pray, is this something that I would feel good about including in my thanksgiving? Or would I be embarrassed to mention it to God? Am I thanking God for this pleasure or have I been enjoying it without ever giving Him a second thought? When we are enjoying legitimate pleasures in a God-honoring way, it seems natural to include them in our prayers. But when we pursue them for their own sake, usually we do not pray about them much at all (or about anything else, for that matter).[1]

These are important questions, for they evaluate whether or not our enjoyments of this life have a

Godward orientation. When our orientation is Godward, it "seems natural" to include the pleasures we enjoy in our prayers. "God, thank you for this meal or this walk in the park. Father, thank you that we can open our windows every morning and let the breeze come through our house. Thank you for this good music or for that recent movie—they were edifying and uplifting and helped me think about good things or helped me understand important realities."

The question of whether or not you can receive an earthly enjoyment with thankfulness is also a question of whether or not you can receive that gift with a *good conscience*. Throughout the New Testament, Paul regularly exhorts Christians to maintain a good conscience (Rom 13:15; 1 Tim 3:9). Indeed, the goal of Paul's entire ministry was to promote a good conscience among professing believers: "But the goal of our instruction is love from a pure heart and a good conscience and a sincere faith" (1 Tim 1:5). A trustworthy test for whether or not we can receive or partake in an earthly enjoyment is whether or not we can thank God for it.

Due to our various backgrounds, we may not be able to receive some legitimate gifts with thanksgiving and a good conscience. For example, before I came to Christ at age nineteen, I immersed myself in all kinds of music. Some of it was innocent, but much of it was immoral and even blasphemous. Almost immediately after I was saved, I became convinced that the *only* music I should listen to is music that is explicitly Christian. It took me a long time before I could listen to any other kind of music with a good conscience.

Today I am now able to listen to music that is not overtly Christian but that is otherwise excellent, wholesome and well-crafted. There were times soon after my conversion, however, that I did listen to music that wasn't explicitly Christian. Looking back, I can see that most of the time, these songs weren't inherently evil. For me, however, I still wasn't able to enjoy this music *with thanksgiving*. I couldn't bless God for the gift of this or that song, yet I partook anyway. This practice defiled my conscience, not because the music was in itself bad, but because I couldn't listen to it with thanksgiving and a good conscience. In other words, I couldn't listen to such songs in faith, and that which is not of faith, as Paul reminds us, is sin (Rom 14:23).

Solomon's command to enjoy life, therefore, is not a wholesale endorsement to indulge our every whim and slake our desires at every turn. We must, as in all of life, maintain a good conscience as we partake in the pleasures God has ordained for our joy. But it is just as important to note that Solomon's exhortations are intended to free us from the oppression of an ill-informed or weak conscience.

Some of us may not be able to see how the vigorous enjoyment of earthly pleasures corresponds with a passionate pursuit of holiness. Yet it is precisely this confusion that Solomon seeks to illuminate. The

Christian life is simultaneously a heavenly life and an earthly life. Yet, even the future life for which we long consists in an eternity of physical existence. Sin will be eradicated, but due to the resurrection, physical realities will not.

What Solomon is pressing upon us is that the physical world matters. Earthly life matters. The body is good. And if you think this is an interpretation merely rooted in the Old Testament, I ask you to consider the resurrection of Jesus Christ. The fact that Jesus Christ rose bodily from the dead demonstrates conclusively that God values the physical world. Jesus has risen from the dead, not merely spiritually, but bodily. The Son of God—get this—will be incarnate for all eternity.

Have you ever pondered this reality? God has bound Himself to His creation forever. And not only this, but we as believers will someday be raised from the dead with new bodies that will live forever, not in an ethereal heaven somewhere out there, but upon a new earth in a sinless, uncorrupted, material universe. Although many people misuse God's earthly gifts and worship the creation rather than the Creator, it does not follow that these earthly gifts cannot be rightly used and enjoyed *in* worshipping the Creator. This earthly life, though tainted by sin and by suffering, enigmas and difficulties, is still a gift. This creation, though fallen, is still good (1 Tim 4:4). If you remove God from life under the sun, nothing matters. That's why Solomon opened his book by saying "vanity of vanities, all is vanity." But if you view life in reference to God, everything matters, including what you eat and drink and enjoy in this life.

Enjoying Life and Loving Our Neighbor

Our neighbor's conscience is also a vital factor to consider as we seek to obey Solomon's Great Commission. It is possible that your fellow brother or sister in Christ is unable to presently partake in particular enjoyments due to *their* background prior to coming to Christ. So important was this issue to the life of the church and the spiritual health of believers that Paul addressed it in detail in two separate places in the New Testament (Rom 14; 1 Cor 8-10). In both cases, there were Christians due to their prior religious experience, who couldn't partake in certain foods.

Depending on a person's religious upbringing, it was possible that prior to Christ they had partaken in overt idol worship. During such worship, meat would be sacrificed to these idols and then later sold in the market. After their conversion, these former idolaters were unable, in good conscience, to eat the meat that had been previously used in idol worship because they believed such an act would dishonor Christ. Paul corrects this wrong thinking by informing his readers that an idol has no actual existence and, therefore, cannot affect the meat one way or another (1 Cor 8:6; 10:26). The meat had come from an animal that God created to be eaten and enjoyed (Gen 9:1-6; Acts 10; 1

Tim 4:4-5); whether it had been used in idol worship had no spiritual significance whatsoever.

The person struggling with whether or not they could eat meat sacrificed to idols had a weak conscience that needed to be informed by these important truths about idols and creation. In its present condition, the weak conscience of this believer was a spiritual liability, and it needed correction. Nevertheless, when it came to whether Paul, the one with a strong conscience on the issue of meat sacrificed to idols, would partake of this God-given enjoyment of a steak dinner in the presence of his brother, Paul always defaulted on the side of love. That is, he would give up his right to enjoy the meat in order to not defile his brother's conscience (1 Cor 10:13).

Our enjoyment of life's good pleasures, therefore, cannot be pursued with a cavalier attitude toward other people. Love for our spiritual siblings prevails over our enjoyment of earthly pleasures. More enjoyable than a filet minion is tasting the love of Christ as we forego legitimate pleasure for the sake our dear brothers and sisters.

A Theology of Earthly Life[2]

When it comes to the matters related to physical life and how Christians should think about earthly enjoyment, the church has rarely found herself securely balanced between the extremes of severe asceticism and unrestrained indulgence. Even the New Testament gives the indication that there has always been pressure to move toward one of these two poles. In Ephesus, there were lovers of pleasure (2 Tim 3:4); in Colossae, there were rigorous ascetics (Col 2:23). In the early church there were those who rejected marriage and some who sought the pseudo-spiritual environment of a monastery. There were the hedonists and the Epicureans. Today we have the legalists and the health, wealth, and prosperity teachers. What we need is a theology of earthly life.

When Paul addresses Timothy on the issue of wealth, he offers counsel that confronts the severe ascetic *and* the unrestrained materialist. Because of the temptations that attended it, great wealth, though not evil in and of itself, is never to be sought or desired (1 Tim 6:9). True godliness will be ever accompanied by contentment (1 Tim 6:6), and those who have significant wealth are to remain humble (1 Tim 6:17a), give generously (1 Tim 6:18), and recognize that God is the ultimate source of all they have (1 Tim 6:17b).

Yet, in case someone might conclude that such warnings against the danger of pursuing wealth imply that God Himself is some sort of Scrooge, unwilling to give His servants even the slightest bit of coal with which to warm themselves, Paul reminds Timothy that it is God who "richly provides us with all things to enjoy" (1 Tim 6:17). The Creator does not dole out meager portions of pleasure to His creatures as though

He were afraid they might get too carried away or deplete the supply; no, He provides *all things richly*.

Solomon's Great Commission and Paul's statement here is a much-needed corrective to those of us who are unable to watch a college football game, eat a juicy steak, or enjoy a good trail run without wondering, at least a little bit, if whether or not we should spend our time on such indulgences. But saying that God provides us richly with all things to enjoy means far more than God providing us with many objects (or experiences) to enjoy.

Real enjoyment of this good creation cannot, as Solomon learned, become detached from a theological context (see Eccl 12:13-14). The attempt to enjoy this world apart from faith and obedience to God will never, by design, lead to abiding satisfaction. We will either gorge ourselves out of fear of future loss, or hesitantly partake of innocent pleasures because we are constantly hounded by a vague sense of guilt. In both cases we have denied the goodness of our Creator.

Order and Proportion

When Jesus told His disciples to shun anxiety by putting their trust in their heavenly Father's promise to provide for all their needs, He summarized His teaching with the memorable statement we read in chapter one: "Seek first the kingdom of God and his righteousness, and all these things will be added unto you" (Matt 6:33). The "all things" refers, as we saw in chapter 2, to the food and clothing He mentioned in the previous verses. Instead of wringing our hands over our daily needs, we can make God and His kingdom the priority of our life because God will see to it that we have everything we need.

But again, this is more than a matter of getting stuff. Jesus is commanding us to set our highest affections upon God so that we might receive the gifts of earthly life in their proper order and proportion. We were made for pleasure—this truth is undeniable. There is futility, as one author has taught us, in "trying to be more spiritual than God."[3] Indeed, as we've learned, the one who denies God's good gifts for the sake of religion may indicate that he is ensnared by the doctrines of demons (see 1 Tim 4:1-5). But Solomon's observations and our own experience tell us that the good things of life *taste their best* when and only when we receive them the way God intended. And we were designed to receive them, not as the main pursuit of life, but as a gracious gift from the One who is the main pursuit of life. "When he loads your table with good things and your cup is overflowing with blessings," Spurgeon reminds us, "rejoice in *him* more than in *them*."[4]

Elsewhere, Solomon says it like this: "The blessing of the LORD makes rich, and he adds no sorrow to it" (Prov 10:22). That is, when, in the course of our diligent pursuit of God, He provides us with things richly to enjoy, these gifts can be received with unhindered delight. On the other hand, unfettered indulgence and reluctant partaking are both the result of pursuing something primarily other than God. In the first case, it is the pursuit of pleasure that has become the first priority; in the second, the pursuit of justification by works has taken root.

Because of God's good gift of creation and His glorious gift of justification by faith alone, Christians are free to enjoy the good things of life *and* free to control ourselves from over-indulging in the good things of life. This will be the mark of spiritual maturity: appreciation for God's goodness and glory in earthly enjoyments, and the ability to receive such pleasures in their right order and proportion. When we "seek first the kingdom of heaven," we will truly "taste and see that the Lord is good" (Ps 34:8).

NOTES

Chapter 1—Solomon's Grand Discovery

1. While the authorship of Ecclesiastes is contended in modern Old Testament scholarship, I believe there is no reason to reject Solomon as the author. For an excellent defense of Solomonic authorship of Ecclesiastes, see William D. Barrick, *Ecclesiastes: The Philippians of the Old Testament*, Focus on the Bible (Ross-shire, Scotland: Christian Focus, 2015), 17-24.

2. Barrick, *Ecclesiastes*, 39.

3. L. Alonso Schokel, *A Manuel of Hebrew Poetics* (Rome: Pontifical Biblical Institute, 1988), 71; quoted in Roland Murphy, *Ecclesiastes*, Word Biblical Commentary (Grand Rapids: Zondervan, 1992), 10.

4. See Michael A. Eaton, *Ecclesiastes*, Tyndale Old Testament Commentaries (Downers Grove, IL: IVP Academic, 1983), 77.

Chapter 2—Solomon's Great Commission: Savor Life Joyfully

1. Sidney Greidanus, *Preaching Christ from Ecclesiastes,* Foundations for Expository Sermons (Grand Rapids: Eerdmans, 2010), 232.

2. Walter Kaiser, *Ecclesiastes: Total Life* (Chicago: Moody Press, 1979), 98.

Chapter 3—Solomon's Great Commission: Celebrate Life Continually

1. Common grace refers to God's kindness to all people during their time on earth, regardless of their present status with Him. While it is true that believers will experience both common grace *and* saving grace, those who are apart from Christ will only experience common grace in this life. Common grace includes earthly blessings that *all people* enjoy but that are distinct from the spiritual blessings that *only believers* enjoy.

2. This section was adapted from Derek Brown, "Say Goodbye to Your Bucket List," at FromTheStudy.com, August 15, 2016, https://fromthestudy.com/2016/04/15/say-goodbye-to-your-bucket-list/.

3. Randy Alcorn, *Happiness* (Carol Stream, IL: Tyndale House, 2015), 392.

4. Douglas Sean O'Donnell, *Ecclesiastes*, Reformed Expository Commentary (Phillipsburg, NJ: P & R, 2014), 179.

5. Michael A. Eaton, *Ecclesiastes*, Tyndale Old Testament Commentaries (Downers Grove, IL: IVP Academic, 1983), 145-46.

6. This section was adapted from Derek Brown, "Christian Dating and Courting: The Question of Physical Attraction," at FromTheStudy.com, August 17, 2017, https://fromthestudy.com/2017/08/11/christian-courting-and-dating-part-3-the-question-of-physical-attraction/

Chapter 4—Solomon's Great Commission: Enjoy Life Thankfully

1. David Gibson, *Living Life Backwards: How Ecclesiastes Teaches Us to Live in Light of the End* (Wheaton, IL: Crossway), 113.

2. It is possible that the intended meaning of Proverbs 12:27 is that the sluggard has refused to either catch or roast his game. The implication is that he fails to take advantage of the abundant opportunities before him to feed himself and enjoy God's provision of food. See Bruce K. Waltke, *The Book of Proverbs: Chapters 1-15*, NICOT (Grand Rapids: Eerdmans, 2004), 542-43.

3. Michael Reeves, *Spurgeon on the Christian Life: Alive in Christ* (Wheaton, IL: Crossway, 2018), 167.

Chapter 5—Solomon's Great Commission: Live Life Purposefully

1. B. B. Warfield, *The Religious Life of Theological Students* (Phillipsburg, NJ: Presbyterian and Reformed, 1911), 182; quoted in Joe Rigney, *The Things of Earth* (Wheaton, IL: Crossway, 2015), 130. By "religion" Warfield means "Christianity," not religion in a generic sense.

2. It has been shown that early retirement can lead to various health problems. "But in our rush to leave the office," Richard W. Johnson writes, "we don't realize that retirement also has a downside, especially over the long term. Many retirees indulge in unhealthy behaviors. They become sedentary and watch too much television. They eat too much. They drink too much. They smoke too much. Without the purpose of fulfilling work, retirees can feel adrift and become depressed. Without the camaraderie of their co-workers, retirees risk becoming

socially isolated. Without the intellectual stimulation that work can provide, retirement can accelerate cognitive decline." See "A Case Against Early Retirement," *The Wall Street Journal*, April 21, 2019.

3.   William D. Barrick, *Ecclesiastes: The Philippians of the Old Testament*, Focus on the Bible (Ross-shire, Scotland: Christian Focus, 2015), 162.

4.   Richard Steele, *The Religious Tradesman* (Harrison, VA: Sprinkle Publications, 1989), 79.

5.   This section is adapted from Derek Brown, "When Your Work is Unfulfilling," in *GraceNotes* 2.4 (Winter 2017), 1.

6.   Steele, *The Religious Tradesman*, 35.

7.   See Matt Perman, *What's Best Next: How the Gospel Transforms the Way You Get Things Done* (Wheaton, IL: Crossway, 2014, 78).

Chapter 6—A Theology of Earthly Life

1.   R. Kent Hughes, *Ecclesiastes: Why Everything Matters*, Preaching the Word (Wheaton, IL: Crossway, 2010), 218.

2.   This last section was adapted from Derek Brown, "All Things Richly: God and the Good Things of Life" at FromTheStudy.com, February 17, 2017, https://fromthestudy.com/2017/02/17/all-things-richly-god-and-the-good-things-of-life/

3.   C. S. Lewis, *Mere Christianity* (San Francisco, HarperSanFrancisco, 1980), 64.

4.   Reeves, *Spurgeon on the Christian Life*, 140.

SCRIPTURE INDEX

ABOUT THE AUTHOR

Originally from Montana, Derek received his bachelor's degree from The Master's University (Santa Clarita, California) and his M.Div. and Ph.D. from The Southern Baptist Theological Seminary (Louisville, Kentucky). He is associate pastor and elder at Creekside Bible Church in Cupertino, California and academic dean at The Cornerstone Bible College and Seminary in Vallejo, California. He lives with his wife and three children in the San Francisco Bay Area.

ABOUT
WITH ALL WISDOM
PUBLICATIONS

With All Wisdom Publications is the book publishing ministry of Creekside Bible Church in Cupertino. We started this publishing ministry out of the simple desire to serve our local body with substantive biblical resources for the sake of our people's growth and spiritual maturity.

But we also believe that book publishing, like any other Christian ministry, should first and foremost be under the supervision and accountability of the local church. While we are grateful for and will continue to support the many excellent traditional publishers available today—our shelves are full of the books they have produced—we also believe that the best place to develop solid, life-giving theology and biblical instruction is within the local church.

With All Wisdom Publications is also unique because we offer our books at a very low cost. We strive for excellence in our writing and seek to provide a high-quality product to our readers. Our editorial team is comprised of men and women who are highly trained and excellent in their craft. But since we are able to avoid the high overhead costs that are typically incurred by traditional publishers, we are able to pass significant savings on to you. The result is a growing collection of books that are substantive, readable, and affordable.

In order to best serve various spiritual and theological needs of the body of Christ, we have developed three distinct lines of books. **Big Truth|little books®** provides readers with accessible, manageable works on theology, Christian living, and important church and social issues in a format that is easy to read and easy to finish. Our **Equip Series** is aimed at Christians who desire to delve a little deeper into doctrine and practical matters of the faith. Our **Foundations Series** is our academic line in which we seek to contribute to the contemporary theological discussion by combining pastoral perspective with rigorous scholarship.

OTHER TITLES FROM
WITH ALL WISDOM
PUBLICATIONS

Please visit us at WithAllWisdom.org
to learn more about these titles

BIG TRUTH little books®
What the Bible Says About Gray Areas
Cliff McManis

Faith: The Gift of God
Cliff McManis

How to Pray for Your Pastor
Derek Brown

The Problem of Evil
Cliff McManis

What the Bible Says About Government
Cliff McManis

God Defines and Defends Marriage
Cliff McManis

Protecting the Flock: The Priority of
Church Membership
Cliff McManis

What the Bible Says About Confrontation
Cliff McManis

Fellowship with God: A Guide to Bible Reading,
Meditation, and Prayer
Derek Brown

What the Bible Says About Hospitality
Cliff McManis

The Danger of Hypocrisy:
Coming to Grips with Jesus'
Most Damning Sermon
J. R. Cuevas

Solomon's Great Commission:
A Theology of Earthly Life
Derek Brown

Equip
The Biblically-Driven Church:
How Jesus Builds His Body
Cliff McManis

God's Glorious Story:
The Truth of What It's All About
Colin Eakin

Strong and Courageous: The Character and Calling of
Mature Manhood
Derek Brown

The Gospel, the Church, and Homosexuality: How the
Gospel is Still the Power of God for
Redemption and Transformation
Edited by Michael Sanelli and Derek Brown

Foundations
Apologetics by the Book
Cliff McManis